THE
50-YARD LINE
MOM®

THE 50-YARD LINE MOM®

ONE MOM'S JOURNEY THROUGH THE NFL AND BEYOND

Jo Ann Pugh

JodyPearl Books
PLANO, TEXAS

© 2017 by Jo Ann Pugh. All rights reserved.

No part of this publication may be reproduced, stored in a retrieval system, or transmitted in any form or by any means, electronic, mechanical, photocopying, recording, or otherwise, without the prior permission of the copyright owner, except in the case of brief quotations embodied in critical articles or reviews and pages where permission is specifically granted by the publisher or author.

Although every precaution has been taken to verify the accuracy of the information contained herein, the author and publisher assume no responsibility for any errors or omissions. No liability is assumed for damages that may result from the use of information contained within.

This book is not intended as a substitute for the medical advice of physicians or financial advice from financial experts.

For special editions or to inquire about bulk discounts, visit **50yardlinemom.com**

ISBN-13: 978-1-97451-653-7

Cover Design: Robin Gilbertson
Interior Design: Gary Rosenberg
Editor: Lesley Marlo
www.ExpertCopy.com

CONTENTS

Acknowledgments 7
Note to the Reader 9
Foreword 11
0 YL • Introduction 15
10 YL • Draft Day 21
20 YL • The Agent 33
30 YL • The NFL Rookie Mom 45
40 YL • The Lifestyle 57
50 YL • The Overnight Celebrity 77
60 YL • NFL Game Day 87
70 YL • The Right Mindset 101
80 YL • The Injured Athlete 109
90 YL • Life After Football 121
100 YL • The Football Network 129
Endnotes 133
About the Author 135

ACKNOWLEDGMENTS

Special thanks to…

My "rock"—my husband of 31 years, Marshall "Chuck" Pugh—for being the best husband and father a woman could ever hope for and for being a devoted spiritual leader for our family.

My daughter, Dominique, an incredibly smart and beautiful young woman. Her knowledge and love of sports are truly inspiring.

My son and the inspiration for this book, Jordan. Watching his dedication to achieving his goals, his unwavering belief in himself, and his commitment to overcoming whatever challenges life throws his way has been one of my great lessons in life.

The two new additions to our family—Jordan's wife, Nikki, and the precious gift she and Jordan have given us, our granddaughter, Lincoln Marie.

THE 50-YARD LINE MOM

Vince Jackson of Marketing Moves, Inc., what can I say? You have been the Pugh family's marketing rock from the day Jordan's NFL career began. You worked with us to develop his brand and website, then moved on to take the 50-Yard Line Mom® from a vision scribbled on a note pad to an established brand. You have been a consummate professional and are a treasured longtime friend to our family. You are a blessing!

Kara Adams, who wove my thoughts, stories, experiences, and advice into a well-crafted narrative...

And to Lesley Marlo, who believed in my vision well before this book was conceived. Lesley and her team at ExpertCopy helped me develop what started as a series of blogs several years ago to this completed work that is my lifelong passion. Lesley joined me on this journey with patience, creativity, encouragement, and the utmost professionalism. Lesley, I am grateful and look forward to our next project.

NOTE TO THE READER

As we journeyed as a family to and through the NFL, I often wished there was a playbook for us to follow. My hope is that our story will help other families chasing big dreams. This book—and our organization, 50-Yard Line Mom®—was created for you and for athletes at all levels of the sports journey to advocate for your financial, physical, and emotional health and well-being.

FOREWORD

NFL 101 is a hard class to master, especially if you're a parent or spouse of a new NFL player. The stakes are high, and there is a ton of pressure. A young player is in uncharted territory and will face a lot of tough decisions—about everything from finances and friends to the sport of football itself. One wrong move—or one bad decision—could change the course of his life.

Football players are expected to perform at their highest level every day. They're asked to commit 100% to the sport, even though they know the average time a player spends in the league is just 3.2 years.

As anyone who has ridden the NFL roller coaster can tell you, the draft is just the beginning. There is so much to learn, and chances are, you and the football player you love will have a lot of questions.

Here are just some of the things I thought about when I first joined the league:

THE 50-YARD LINE MOM

How will I make my mark in this sport?

How do I handle the celebrity and fame?

Who has my best interest at heart?

Who can I trust?

Do the coaches want me or not?

What will happen to me if I get injured?

Will the NFL take care of me long-term if I'm injured and can't play?

What should I know about concussions?

Am I living above my means?

Who can help answer these questions for me?

The choices new players must make can be overwhelming. They need help and guidance in making them. Unfortunately, there's no handbook for parents or spouses of players, so most players and their families are left to figure it out on their own through trial and error.

Professional football is a tough business. It can eat you alive, paralyze you, and even make you question your sanity at times! My family and I really didn't know what I was getting into when I was selected in the NFL draft. I can't tell you what a difference it would have made if we'd had a resource like this book to help us.

As the mother of a former player, Jo Ann Pugh

FOREWORD

knows firsthand how unpredictable and rocky the NFL journey can be. She's been through it all with her son, Jordan, and she's well-equipped to make it easier for you to navigate what may, at times, seem like a minefield.

So listen up, and pay close attention! In the following pages, Jo will tell you what you need to know to be prepared for your own NFL adventure. Only experience can edify, so I implore you to use hers. It is tried and true.

—*Eugene Robinson*

During his 16-year career playing free safety in the NFL, Eugene Robinson was named to the Pro Bowl roster three times and was part of the Green Bay Packers' Super Bowl XXXI championship over the New England Patriots.

INTRODUCTION

"I prayed for this child, and the Lord has granted what I asked of Him."
—1 SAMUEL 1:27[1]

My son Jordan's path to the NFL began on a beach in Sandestin, Florida, when he was eight years old. My husband, Chuck, and I had taken our two children–Jordan, and his younger sister, Dominique–on a family vacation to enjoy the Florida sunshine and shoreline. The kids were loving every minute of it.

As Chuck and I stretched out in the sand, I watched Jordan dashing in and out of the waves, so full of energy and boyish exuberance. He was a wisp of a boy with a short little body and long, lanky arms, and at the time, he was the shortest boy in his class. My little string bean. But that little boy had big dreams, as Chuck and I were about to find out.

THE 50-YARD LINE MOM

Jordan raced over to us, struck his best bodybuilder pose, and smiled. "I want to be an NFL player," he announced.

Chuck shot me a glance, and I knew what he was thinking. *"This tiny little thing playing in the NFL?"* It didn't seem possible.

And I admit, my first thought after Jordan shared his plans was, *"God bless you. I'm going to pray for you, son."*

But that's not what I said. I told him that he could do whatever he wanted in life, and in the meantime, he needed to focus on his studies. The truth was that while I'd always support Jordan's dreams, I didn't really *believe* he'd make it.

You have to understand…

I'm very analytical. I believe the proof is in the data. There are thousands of young boys across America who dream of playing in the NFL. But here's the cold, hard truth:

- 1,121,744 boys play high school football
- 1 in 40 high school players will play in college
- 1 in 1,010 high school players will be drafted to the NFL
- 1 in 325 college players will be drafted to the NFL

I didn't know the stats that day on the Florida beach. I just knew that playing for the NFL was a long shot.

I'm not sharing these numbers in an attempt

INTRODUCTION

to dash anyone's dreams. But they illustrate how difficult it is to ascend to the professional ranks. My job as a mom was not to crush my son's dreams, it was to balance reality. As young as he was, however, Jordan knew what needed to be done, and he did it. He knew he needed to be physically strong, so he worked on getting stronger, doing 200 pushups every night. We could hear him as he counted off his pushups from downstairs in our house... 1, 2, 3, 4...

Jordan also knew he needed to be fast. We didn't allow him to go far from our house, so Jordan ran from the stop sign at one end of our street to the stop sign at the other end. Back and forth, back and forth, back and forth.

One of our neighbors remembered seeing young Jordan running up and down our street, over and over. "I would see him running back and forth, and thought to myself, *'Boy, isn't he special,'*" he told me when Jordan was drafted. He had no clue that Jordan was running all those sprints with one goal in mind: to run fast enough to one day play in the NFL.

There was one brief moment when I thought Jordan might give up. He fell on the field and cut himself during a youth football game on the east side of town and started screaming, "Blood! Blood! Blood!"

"Well, now I don't have to worry about him playing football since he's freaking out over a little bit of blood," I thought.

But it made Chuck so angry. He yelled, "Boy, if you don't get up off that ground!"

THE 50-YARD LINE MOM

Jordan did as he was told. When his fear of blood didn't stop him, I knew Jordan was determined to play football. But even then, it still wasn't really registering with me that he could make it a reality, even though we had athletes in our family. My husband played high school football, but he quit college ball after about a day because the other kids were too big.

My great uncle, James "Buster" Clarkson, played professional baseball in the Negro leagues. In Puerto Rico's winter league, he played with Satchel Paige. Buster's teammates also included Roberto Clemente and Willie Mays. After Major League Baseball was integrated, he had a short stint playing for the Boston Braves, debuting as a rookie at the age of 37 in the 1951 season.

The possible reality of Jordan's dream only started to sink in after an invitation to the Nike football camp and one particularly standout performance on the football field during Jordan's senior year in high school. Jordan's team, Plano West, was facing off against Flower Mound, a particularly tough opponent. Jordan played offense during that game. After the game, three of Jordan's coaches came up to my husband and I and said they had never seen a performance like that. The head football coach even apologized, saying, "I have underutilized Jordan all of these years, and I am sorry."

The week prior to the Flower Mound game, Jordan made the paper for another outstanding performance and team win. "South Garland Got Pughed," the headline read. The following spring, Jordan got

INTRODUCTION

32 scholarship offers! That's when I finally thought, *"There might be something to this football dream after all."*

I wrote this book as a player mom for other player moms. Moms whose sons have a gift and a love for football and who just might have a shot at going pro. If you're one of those moms, I'm pretty sure I know the questions that run through your mind.

How do we get to the professional ranks?

And more importantly, how do I get my son all the way through the process so that after his NFL career is over, he emerges as a well-rounded individual?

This is the journey that our family took to get through the NFL season of our lives with our son, Jordan. I hope hearing about our experience, the lessons we learned, and the advice we offer in these pages will help you be better prepared to embark on the journey to and through professional sports with your own son or daughter.

Blessings,
Jo Ann Pugh
The 50-Yard Line Mom®

The mission of 50-Yard Line Mom® is to share insights and advice that will have a significant influence on the development of kids throughout their sports journey. The goal is to impact individuals and the industry as a whole in a positive way and to help parents raise physically, emotionally, and financially strong young people.

DRAFT DAY

- *About 6.5%, or approximately one in 16, of all high school senior boys playing interscholastic football will go on to play football at a National Collegiate Athletic Association (NCAA) member institution.*

- *Less than two in 100, or 1.6%, of NCAA senior football players will get drafted by a National Football League (NFL) team.*

- *Eight in 10,000, or approximately 0.08%, of high school senior boys playing interscholastic football will eventually be drafted by an NFL team.[2]*

DRAFT DAY EXPECTATIONS

When most people think of the NFL Draft, they think of those players who fly up to New York City surrounded by loads of media coverage. Players imagine their names will be called by the NFL Commissioner, they will hug their families and then don their new team's hat and jersey amid all the lights and applause.

That experience happens for only a select few high-profile players who were actively recruited. Just a handful. For most players, draft day will be spent at home, surrounded by family and friends, watching the coverage on ESPN and NFL Network. And that's how it was for us. We may not have had all the fanfare, but there was a festive mood in our house. We were excited!

My son, Jordan, had worked so hard for so many years, and now he was on the verge of realizing his life's dream–playing in the NFL. We had a house full of family and friends from near and far to support Jordan. His best friend from high school came into town. His buddies from Texas A&M University in College Station were all camped out at our house. Everyone wanted to be part of the celebration.

The weather was beautiful that weekend, but no one wanted to be outside. All eyes were glued to the television. The draft began on Thursday and would last for three days. As it got started, the mood in our house was lighthearted and fun. Because Jordan wasn't expected to be a first- or second-round draft pick, we could relax and enjoy that first night with no pressure.

The truth is that Jordan didn't receive a lot of positive feedback in the months leading up to the draft. He didn't get invited to the Senior Bowl or the

DRAFT DAY

NFL Combine, and that's where he would have had the best platform to show off his talents. Still, Jordan did work out for several teams. One of the scouts told Jordan that the best he could expect was to enter the league as a free agent. In fact, this scout recommended that Jordan *not* watch the draft because it would be very disappointing for him. There was no way that was going to happen, no matter how things turned out. We were filled with pride over how much Jordan had accomplished, and we made sure he knew it.

Things started looking up that first evening when the Kansas City Chiefs called Jordan. They said, "Be prepared for day two. We will probably take you in the third or fourth round." He heard similar from a few other teams, so we were all excited and anxious going into day two.

Friday seemed to drag on endlessly. We listened as name after name was called. But not Jordan's name. He watched as a number of defensive backs got drafted, but not him. And that was his position.

By 8 p.m., we were concerned. As a mother, I was starting to hurt for my son. We remained hopeful that Saturday would bring good news, but the mood in our house had definitely changed.

Coverage began early Saturday morning. The fifth round of the draft came and went. Now it was the sixth round, and by noon, Jordan was disappointed, angry, and frustrated. He still hadn't been selected. The draft was entering the middle to end picks in the sixth round.

THE 50-YARD LINE MOM

My husband and I prayed. We called on the Lord. We asked Him why.

My son had been the model athlete. He was never in trouble. He was obedient and respectful to his parents. He studied hard. He graduated in three-and-a-half years from business school at one of the top academic universities in the state of Texas. He completed his college pro day with stats that beat many of the stats of athletes who went to the NFL Combine.

But on that day, the final day of the draft, he continued to see other players get drafted over him. My husband and I asked God through prayer, "What in the world is going on?"

Chuck and I raised our son to trust in God and to believe that through Jesus Christ all things are possible. We taught him that what matters most is your faith, your character, and then, your hard work. I had shared with my son early in his life that I felt God had a special calling for him. As I watched my son's disappointment grow with every name called, I felt that we had been let down.

My husband and I called Jordan to the bedroom to talk to him, away from his friends. He had tears in his eyes. He just didn't understand. He had worked so hard and done everything right. All we could say to him was, "Jordan, we don't know what to tell you. But if football is God's plan for you, it's going to happen."

Throughout our conversation, Jordan kept looking at his phone. He was waiting for the call. The call he'd been waiting for since he was a young boy on the beach with a dream. The call that would welcome him into the NFL. He had waited so long, worked so hard, was so close, and it looked like the call wasn't going to come. Still, Jordan was fixated on that phone.

"Being drafted is something that you do not have control over," Chuck told Jordan. "It's a waiting game, plain and simple.

"Give us your cellphone. Your mom and I want you to go take a walk. Get out of the house. Get away from your friends, and go down to the lake."

From our house, it's a five-minute walk to the lake in our subdivision. It has a gorgeous fountain that sprays water up and into a large pond. Ducks gather to swim and waddle around the grounds around the water. The lake is surrounded by walking trails situated under large shade trees and lush landscaping. It's like a movie set of where you would go to have a heart-to-heart talk with God. Jordan reluctantly gave us his phone and left the house. I bet you can figure out what happened next.

He had not been gone five minutes when the phone rang.

"Is Jordan there? This is the General Manager of the Carolina Panthers."

My heart raced. Jordan only had five minutes to accept the offer, and the clock was ticking. I didn't know it at the time, but unless the GM talked to Jordan, he would not be drafted. I muted the phone and yelled, "Chuck, jump in the truck and go down there and try to find him!"

I stalled on the phone while Chuck rushed down to the lake in his truck. I got back on the phone with the GM. "He's coming. He's coming. *Jordan!*" I called, knowing full well that Jordan was not in the house, nor could he hear me.

"Ma'am, we have to talk to him. We only have five minutes on the clock," said the voice on the other end of the phone.

"He's coming, he's coming," I said, less convincing with each passing minute.

I don't know how he did it, but Chuck got Jordan back to the house within five minutes. He jumped out of the truck and grabbed the phone from me.

"Jordan, this is the GM with the Carolina Panthers. How is your day going?"

"It hasn't been going real well. I haven't been drafted yet," Jordan said.

"Well, we're going to change that. We're drafting you."

Well, let me tell you, we all went nuts. We were screaming and so happy, relieved that Jordan finally got the call. He was an NFL draft pick.

Ten minutes later, the Dallas Cowboys called.

"Jordan, are you still on the board?"

"No, sir, the Carolina Panthers just picked me up."

Not one team, but two teams called to draft him. Jordan was elated.

In all the commotion of scrambling to find Jordan

when the Panthers called, we missed seeing his photo and information displayed on ESPN when they finally announced his name. Thankfully, a family friend took a picture of the television screen when Jordan was selected.

> Jordan Pugh, sixth-round draft pick for the Carolina Panthers.

After the excitement about being drafted had died down a bit, Jordan and I spoke about his quiet time by the lake. "I walked down to the lake and sat down on the bench," Jordan said. "I bowed my head in prayer and said, 'I'm done. I've done everything I can do. I'm done. I want You to take over. Whatever it is that You want me to do, Lord, I will do.'"

Jordan said the moment he finished saying that prayer is when his dad appeared in the truck, honking the horn and yelling for him to get in.

To this day, when Jordan speaks about being drafted, he tells that story about talking to God.

PREPARE YOUR SON FOR DRAFT DAY

Since the draft day experience is unpredictable and completely out of your control, how do you help your son get through it? The best way to prepare your son for the NFL Draft is to help him set realistic expectations. It doesn't dampen the dream, but it lessens the blow if he doesn't get the outcome he wants.

THE 50-YARD LINE MOM

If your son is being very highly recruited, he is the flagship of the college team, and they've got him blasted all over the place in the media, then it may be reasonable to expect that he will go early in the draft. He might be that player who flies to New York City. But I think even then, you should temper those expectations. Chances are that your son will indeed get drafted, but chances are even greater that it's not going to be a flashy, red-carpet experience.

Jordan had worked out all spring. He'd been working with a trainer two or three times a day, getting his body strong and preparing to show his skills to NFL scouts.

Even though he'd already graduated from Texas A&M, Jordan was able to attend the school's pro day. The NFL scouts who were there that day said things like, "Where did this kid come from?" They couldn't believe his performance. That positive feedback got Jordan pumped up. Three or four scouts, including one from Chicago and another from Kansas City, told Jordan he would probably go in the third or fourth round of the draft. That was all the motivation Jordan needed to hear. He continued his workouts with even more focus and determination. It seemed that his dream was within reach.

When I think about that time, I remember the mix of emotions that I experienced—everything from disbelief to gratitude that Jordan had this opportunity, to frustration and anger that he wasn't being selected after all his hard work. When I encountered negative

DRAFT DAY

feelings about the draft process, I had to take a step back and remind myself that it was an honor to even be in this position. There are thousands of talented kids out there who will never get this chance.

It's a stressful experience for everyone, but you have to remain calm. My sense of peace came from my faith. I know that not everyone believes in God or has faith, but I don't know how I would have gotten through something like this without it. Without our faith, it would have been overwhelming for Jordan, and for us, to process all the feelings involved, especially the depression, anger, and frustration.

The NFL Draft is just one moment in time. If your son doesn't get the result he had hoped for, it doesn't mean that his NFL dream is over, as long as he keeps fighting for it. I advised Jordan to focus on becoming a free agent if he didn't get drafted. Many players join the league as free agents, including a close friend who ended his pro career as one of football's best players. Sharing other players' success stories with your son will help him stay focused, and it will give him hope. Not being drafted isn't necessarily the end of his dream.

I won't lie to you. That whole experience was really, really hard. And now that I look back on it, the draft prepared us for the reality of the NFL—the disappointments, the things you think aren't fair, the stress, the emotional ups and downs.

It was a hard time, but the draft was just the beginning of our NFL journey.

THE 50-YARD LINE MOM

DRAFT DAY ADVICE

The most important advice I can give is to make the circle of people around you on draft day really, really small. You'll see huge draft day parties on TV with dozens of people at the house, and I strongly advise against that. Only invite people who have actually been involved in your son's life and have his best interests in mind. I can't stress this point enough.

It is amazing how many people will want to be a part of your draft day festivities. I think they want to be a part of this celebrity athlete's inner circle, and they want a front-row seat. If the draft doesn't go as you had hoped, a large group of supporters can become a distraction for your son. It's probably more challenging to keep the atmosphere positive, upbeat, and encouraging when there is a group larger than 10 or so people. Some people may tease your son or be so vocal with their opinions that it may create a very negative environment. Plus, it may not be easy to pull your son away from a large group to get some quiet time for reflection and encouragement in private, if needed.

One person I would discourage you from inviting is your son's agent. I think the draft needs to be a private moment shared with close family and friends. Jordan's agent wasn't invited to watch the draft with us, but he did come over afterward. The moment when Jordan got the call that he was drafted into the NFL was reserved for family and close friends.

DRAFT DAY

There's one more thing you should know about draft day, and I will give my daughter, Dominique, credit for this realization: As a family, you'll feel like you were drafted, too. You'll experience every emotion your son does. Maybe in a different form, but all the highs and lows, the disappointment, the frustration, the elation...

If you are actively engaged in your son's career, those emotions will continue. Welcome to life in the NFL.

THE AGENT

Are agents really necessary? With the 2011 Collective Bargaining Agreement, rookie contracts are for the most part standard with established value on every draft pick.[3]

SELECTING AN AGENT

Entering his senior year of college, your son dreams of becoming a professional athlete. He has incredible athletic ability and a phenomenal season. He has ambition and works hard on his skills on and off the field. His name begins to appear on lists of draft prospects. Invitations start to roll in for the Senior Bowl, the NFL Combine, and pro days at his college. What your son doesn't have is an agent.

Choosing a great agent is very important as your son works to enter the professional football league. Professional football is part of the entertainment industry, bottom line. It doesn't matter if you're a musician, an actor, or athlete—if you are in entertainment, you need a great agent. And once it becomes a real possibility that your son is going to be part of this exclusive club, it's easy to get caught up in the excitement.

Your son may be thinking, *"Wow! I'm in demand and popular. I am a celebrity."* And you may get caught up in all the hype as well. You may be in awe that your son is even being considered for an opportunity to go to the pros. I know I was. It's the equivalent of a modern fairy tale for boys.

Playing professional sports is the number one fantasy of most little boys. *Enjoy it.* It's a magical time that most athletes and their families will never get to experience, but you have to keep your wits about you.

Agents make contact while you're in the midst of pre-draft euphoria, and you may not be thinking about what the agent-player relationship means long-term. This relationship is too important to be based on how well your family is wined and dined, the gifts you receive, or the promises of how things will be. To pick an agent well, you need to make an informed decision based on references, knowledge, and research.

Remember, professional football is a business, and you need to make sure your son's interests are the top priority. Most NFL rookies have an agent their first year in the league. Selecting the *right* agent for your son is what you need to focus on. Sports agents serve a valuable role for professional athletes

THE AGENT

by guiding their decisions and negotiating their contracts. The challenge is finding an agent that really has your son's best interests at heart. It takes a lot of weeding through to find the right one.

Some agents are only focused on the money and their own self-promotion. Agents have their place, but even a great agent needs to be held accountable and work hard for his most important client—your son.

When I say it is difficult, I mean it is *extremely* difficult to weed out those agents who are trying to get all of the player's money. Agents are limited in how much they are allowed to charge for negotiating their clients' NFL contracts. They're only allowed 3% of the contract.

Players' base salaries are also set by the NFL, so what does an agent actually do for your son to justify receiving 3% of his contract? You need to ask yourself this question, and you have the right to do so. In my opinion, the primary responsibility of an agent is to negotiate the best NFL contract for your son.

When our family went through this process, there wasn't much education or advice for college athletes and their parents when it came to choosing an agent who would work on our behalf. While agents are looking to sign the best talent to their rosters, players need to evaluate prospective agents just as closely. Your son needs someone skilled and respected to help propel his career to the next level. An agent should possess and provide proof of the following skill set: strong negotiation skills, legal background, effective interpersonal skills, an understanding of your family's unique needs, and a strong network of industry contacts.

Start by asking for recommendations from the people you already know. Talk with professional and college athletes, scouts, and coaches to get information about the agents you are considering and what kind of reputation the agent has in the league. You have to ask a lot of questions. Based on the feedback from your connections, narrow down the list of prospective agents and then do additional research. You're looking for someone who has a track record of helping athletes in a similar position. You also want representation from someone who will be available to you when you need him or her. An agent with a long list of clients may be too busy, while an agent with a very short client list could potentially be too inexperienced.

Once you have a short list of agents you are considering, meet with each candidate face to face. There is no better way to gauge how your son, your family, and the agent will gel as a team. Ask potential agents what they know about your son. You should expect each agent to come to the meeting prepared, knowing your son's professional bio, stats, and personal interests. The agent must understand what your son's goals are and the best way to help him attain them.

Find out if the agent is open to being accountable. Let him know that if promises are made, you will expect follow through. Ask a range of questions. What is the usual agent-player relationship? How often will he or she and your son talk or meet? How long will it take to have a phone call returned? What types of services are offered and for what fees? How does the agent divide time among his various clients? If there is more than one agent in the firm, who will be your son's "point person"? Has the agent been fired by an athlete before? Ask what the player would say was the reason the agent was fired. Ask to talk to the agent's current and former clients.

PLAYERS BEWARE! DON'T ENTER THE LEAGUE IN DEBT TO YOUR AGENT

You may be familiar with the stories of NFL players who don't have money when they leave the league. One reason is that some young men enter the league already in debt to their agent. As crazy as it may sound, it happens because some agents will give prospective players loans prior to signing their NFL contract.

About three years ago, I got a call from a mother whose son had been a rookie with the Dallas Cowboys. She was referred to me by the agent representing Jordan at the time. The agent reached out to me first and said, "The kid's not my client right now. Obviously, I'd like to have this player as a client, but I want you to talk to his mother about his situation. I know you are passionate about helping these young men."

THE 50-YARD LINE MOM

This young man was a pretty high-profile player who had unfortunately gotten into some trouble and was no longer a part of the Cowboys organization. The mother said, "I don't know what to do. My son has gotten in a little trouble, but now I have this agent calling. He's talking about they want to sue us because my son owes them money."

"Owes money?" I said, incredulous. I was shocked.

"They gave him a loan before he signed his NFL contract and now they want him to pay it back," she explained. "About fifty-thousand dollars that they loaned him so he could buy a new car, clothes, and an apartment."

Imagine if this was your son! He hadn't signed an NFL contract. He hadn't played a single down of professional football. Anything can happen before you sign, whether you are a first-round draft pick or not, and your son may never get the big payday he thinks is a sure thing. Taking a loan from an agent is spending money your son doesn't have and money he may never get.

YOU DECIDE WHAT THE AGENT DOES FOR YOU

You should also consider how many hats you'd like the agent to wear. Should the agent who negotiates your son's contract also be his business manager? What about his marketing manager or financial planner? Does this create a conflict?

THE AGENT

Regardless of how many different roles your agent has, your son should be involved in EVERY aspect of his own career. Your son's agent should *never* have the authority to do anything on his behalf without your son's approval.

Agents make the majority of their money from other services they try to include in the contract. For example, some agents will charge 25% of the contract for marketing opportunities. If your son is a high-profile player like Cam Newton, Von Miller, or Peyton Manning, for example, how much marketing work does an agent really have to do? Companies and brands actively solicit these select players to endorse their products, make personal appearances, and so on.

I shared my thoughts about marketing opportunities with the agents we considered. I told them we wanted them to bring us marketing opportunities, but we would negotiate those on a case-by-case basis. Does an agent need to get fair compensation? Absolutely. But I didn't want to pay an agent 25% for something he really didn't work to do.

If your son is a first-round draft pick, he doesn't need anyone marketing for him. The opportunities will come to him. What he would really need in that situation is an attorney to look at the agreement, not an agent taking 25% and then an attorney taking his or her cut as well.

As you select an agent, it's important for your son, as well as the family, to "click" with the agent. Jordan was approached by a series of different agents over the course of his NFL career. One agent, a pretty high-profile agent, we felt wasn't right because he was known to lavishly wine and dine young prospects and bring lots of women around. We cut that off because it was not a good fit for us.

Another agent was really just trying to build up his clientele and business. I spent more time helping his business by referring contacts to him than he spent working on activities that would benefit Jordan. He was just too inexperienced to be a good fit for us.

Then we finally found an agent with whom we really connected. He understood our family. I truly believed that this agent had my son's best interests at heart, but we had to work through other agents to get there. So it's okay to select carefully and change agents if necessary. You can start out signing with an agent full of great expectations for a good relationship, but if it doesn't work out, I'm here to tell you and your son that it's okay to fire your agent and get another one.

WORKING WITH AN AGENT

Being successful in the NFL requires more than just knowing the team playbook. Your son has to know about the business side of professional football.

Think about the stories you hear about an agent-client relationship that has gone sour. Maybe the agent didn't work on the player's behalf, or the agent took something from the athlete. An agent

THE AGENT

may get a player signed to an $80 million contract, and then ten years later, the player is broke. It could be the agent's fault, or it could be the client's fault, because some agents give really good advice that their clients don't take.

When Jordan was looking for an agent, most agents wanted full control over his contract. Basically, those agents' mindset was, "I'm going to handle the contract, and you just sign it." They wanted to be his marketing manager so they could go out and market him. If they didn't want to be Jordan's financial advisor too, the agents wanted to bring in someone who was part of their group to give Jordan advice on how to invest his money.

One agent told us about one of his high-profile clients whom he put on a budget. The agent sent this player a check with his spending money every month. I was shocked. The player didn't pay for anything. He didn't write a check for the light bill. He didn't write a check for the rent.

When an agent handles all the money, it is *not* in the player's best interest. Too many entertainers and athletes find their money stolen and are left penniless because they don't sign their own checks.

It has been my experience that you have to clearly define what the agent's role is going to be. *"First of all, Mr. Agent, I want you to negotiate the best contract you can on Jordan's behalf. Jordan will not sign anything until he has read it, all of it, and understood every word. And Jordan will have input on the contract from his parents."*

THE 50-YARD LINE MOM

Ask to see the contract. Some agents don't even want to show the players the contract. They want the players to go on faith. I wanted Jordan to see his contract. So I said, "Jordan we are going to sit down together. You are going to read this contract. If you have any questions on any element of the contract, ask your agent to explain it."

Many agents don't want the players to ask questions. But as an informed mom, you need to make sure your son signs with an agent who is willing to be transparent, helpful, and accountable.

"Mr. Agent, you will not be Jordan's marketing manager. You will not be Jordan's financial advisor. As his agent, you can have some input, but Jordan can find objective sources for those types of services."

Many agents don't like hearing these limitations. So you can weed out a number of agents with these simple stipulations. Remember, the agent should be your son's contract negotiator, NOT the financial advisor who establishes your son's budget, nor the person signing his checks and paying his bills. Your son must be engaged and involved in all decisions regarding his career and his finances.

Sitting down with the agent and asking questions you or your son have is so important. Every month, Jordan and I had a meeting or conference call with his agent. We would set the agenda for the meeting and send it out prior to the call. It was an opportunity for Jordan to learn from his agent what he needed to do to have continued success in the NFL, know what his status was with the team and

THE AGENT

within the league, and be involved in promoting his career. I strongly advise every player and his mom to do the same thing every month.

Both Jordan and his agent were held accountable for a successful relationship. The main point of the meeting or call was to find out what the agent had been doing in the past 30 days. In short, what was he doing to earn his fee? We had these types of meetings with every NFL agent Jordan had over the years. Over time, Jordan was driving the meetings with the agent. He was confident and could speak his mind, ask his questions, and demand answers. We had one agent who wasn't up to the task. Eventually, that agent was fired for not having a plan or a way to fulfill his promises.

Your son needs to know that he is entitled to certain benefits. He needs to know that he has certain rights. Acting on your son's behalf to establish an effective agent relationship is one of the most critical responsibilities a player's mom has.

It's about being an advocate for your son, but you can only do that if you educate yourself enough to know what questions to ask and what knowledge to share.

If needed, I didn't mind being in the role as the mother from hell or as a momma bear protecting her cub. This allows your son to be the "good guy" in the agent relationship, while you can be the "bad guy." Being strong, firm, and assertive was a reminder to the agent that I had a watchful eye on what he was doing for my son. I tried to balance that because there has to be a positive working relationship.

When Jordan and I talked on the phone, he would let me know how he wanted me to be involved.

"Mom, I want you to be there with the agent when we're discussing this."

"OK, Jordan, how far do you want me to go with this?"

"Mom, I want you take the lead."

"OK, then you're not doing this, this, or this, and your agent needs to tell us why he thinks we should. If we can't come to an agreement, then you need to call him back and tell him we're done."

Close involvement in agent relations really gave Jordan the sense that he had a solid understanding of the business side of football and that he knew exactly what was going on with his career.

Remember, you need to establish ground rules and create expectations right up front about the kind of agent-player relationship your family wants. It's about making the agent accountable and a partner in your son's success in the league.

And if you encounter an agent who is not really trying to keep the family and the player together, but instead is trying to push you all apart, run away from that agent as fast as you can.

THE NFL ROOKIE MOM

Mother Demands $1 Million from NFL Son.[4]

DON'T LEAVE OUT THE SIBLINGS

So your son has realized his dream. He's a professional athlete. You've done an awesome job of encouraging and supporting your son up to this point, but your job is far from over.

Your son still needs you as his advocate, cheerleader, and biggest fan. There is so much to learn about the professional football league, but there are a few key points I want you to consider at the very beginning.

Because of the glare of being in the spotlight, an NFL athlete becomes used to having the attention focused solely on him. And unfortunately, family and friends can inadvertently buy into that. It's a constant struggle for any parent to successfully balance the needs of all her children, but it's even more

THE 50-YARD LINE MOM

challenging when one of your kids is a professional athlete. When I think about whether there is something that I could have done a little bit better during our journey to and through the NFL, it would be better parenting of my child who was not a celebrity. When you have a high-profile child, the other siblings may sometimes feel like they're being left out. To be honest, many times they are.

When Jordan would call, I would stop what I was doing to address what it was that he was calling about, whether it was regarding an injury or about his playing time. I didn't realize at the time how much of my time supporting his career was taking. If we went home for a family reunion, all the relatives would flock to Jordan, and that left his sister over to the side by herself.

I don't know how you address that other than to try to make your other children feel special in their own way. I think maybe I spent more time with Jordan than I should have. In retrospect, I could have spent more time with Dominique. I think there were times she resented all that attention devoted to Jordan and his career. I don't blame her, but I really don't know how you change it. You do everything that you can to keep the other child included, but even so, there is always sibling rivalry. I have three siblings, and each one of us feels like another one got more attention growing up. I think it's just part of being a sibling.

Once Jordan started playing in the pros, we allowed Dominique space to get out from under

Jordan's constant shadow. Dominique was now a young adult, so we would allow her to stay home if she didn't want to go to Jordan's games. When she was younger, we didn't give her a choice. If Jordan had a game when he was in high school and college, then Dominique had to go. Staying together as a family at that time was important to us. We loosened the reins as she matured to allow her the opportunity to pursue her own interests.

On Friday nights during the season, my husband and I would try to do something special with Dominique, like take her out to dinner before we would leave to attend Jordan's game on Sunday. Then she would go stay with her cousins for a sleepover, shopping, movies, or just to hang out with them.

When Jordan came home, he had to follow our rules. With us, he wasn't the superstar. *"You're going to take out the trash just like everybody else. You're going to clean up after yourself. Even though you are a professional football player, there's no hanging out until 4 or 5 o'clock in the morning."*

We wanted to make sure that Dominique could see that we still expected Jordan to live by our house rules and that he didn't get special treatment just because he played professional football. Of course, we would try to keep things normal, but then we'd go out to dinner and people would be gathering around Jordan asking for his autograph. So much for saying he wasn't special.

The advice I'd give to any parent going through this: Do the best you can. Then, forgive yourself.

And use my experience as a reminder to give more time and attention to your children who are not celebrities.

KEEP THE INNER CIRCLE SMALL

Now that your son is a professional athlete, he may be getting more media attention, and people on the street may start to recognize him. It will be important for him to remember his celebrity status when he encounters new people in his life. It will be harder to discern if these new people are interested in befriending the NFL player or the man who happens to be an NFL player.

"No New Friends" is a policy some people implement to address this concern. If new people are allowed into the athlete's life at all, it's either very difficult or very rare.

Other athletes swear by the mantra "Trust No One." Because so many people who befriend rookie players have a hidden agenda, it's often difficult to discern upfront who is trustworthy and who is not. Some may find it easier just to assume the worst of everyone.

I think it may be more appropriate to "Be Leery of Everyone." When your son becomes a celebrity, the new people coming into his life should have to prove that they are trustworthy. That may be different from everyday life, where we typically give people the benefit of the doubt until they prove otherwise. As a celebrity, it is totally the opposite.

THE NFL ROOKIE MOM

I used to tell Jordan that the people who were with him those first couple of years in college were probably going to be his true friends. And there's just a handful of them. When Jordan got into the NFL, he may have made one or two friends, but friendships became more of a challenge because fellow players and teammates were now his competition.

Your son has to keep that in mind. Everyone on the field is trying to retain his spot on the team's 53-man roster. Your son may have one or two friends who he will meet in that very early stage of making the team, and they may stay friends for a very long time. But after the initial few weeks on the team, he probably won't make as many friends. There is so much change in personnel with players getting injured, cut, traded, and leaving the league.

Fortunately, Jordan was not really all that social like his sister, Dominique, who is a social butterfly. Jordan kept to himself more, so I don't think it was very difficult for him to keep his inner circle small. Maybe I made him a tiny bit paranoid in thinking that everybody wanted something. He would often ask me, "Do you have to think everyone has to be after something?"

"Well, to be honest, most of them are," I would say time and time again.

In my opinion, the best way for your son to feel comfortable with the people in his life is to keep his inner circle very, very, very, *very* tight.

THE 50-YARD LINE MOM

IT'S NOT YOUR MONEY. IT'S YOUR SON'S MONEY

When a young man gets drafted into professional sports, his family often thinks they've hit the jackpot. They come out of the woodwork asking for money. The newly perceived-to-be rich athlete can feel pressured or obligated to give in to the demands for money, or he may even be made to feel guilty when he does not give in to such requests. But it's the player's money to do with as he pleases.

It's not your money. It's your son's money.

There was a case in the news about a former first-round NFL Draft pick whose mother demanded $1 million from him after he was drafted. She sued him, saying she spent 18 years raising him and was entitled to a payday for doing so. I don't know this young man or his mother, but in my experience, her request isn't all that unusual. It's just a bit extreme.

Moms, you probably do deserve a million dollars for all that work you put into your son's life. I know I feel like no one can pay me what I feel like I'm worth to my son. I worked extremely hard and sometimes worked two jobs in order to do what I did for Jordan. I sacrificed a lot to pour money and time into him. But even still, I'm not entitled to his money, and he is not obligated to repay me.

Do I hope that he will appreciate all my sacrifices and do little things for me and his family? Absolutely. But if he doesn't, it's his money. He can do

THE NFL ROOKIE MOM

with it what he thinks is best. I would hope that I have raised a son that would think of others and not be selfish or self-centered. But even if that's the case, I am still not entitled to his money.

I think the only thing that a professional athlete owes his parents is respect and gratitude for the support, sacrifice, and encouragement the parents provided over the years. The player's success—the ability to take care of himself—is one of the greatest gifts a child can give his parents.

I never wanted my son to feel obligated to help me financially. Instead, I'd rather have him *want* to help me if it was needed. I'm not going to ask Jordan for things because I worked every day so I wouldn't need his money. Plus, it freed me to be able to tell him exactly what I think, because I wasn't dependent on his money and wasn't concerned about staying in his good graces.

Over the years, players have told me that I wouldn't believe what people ask them for—ranging from cousins calling to ask for money to get their hair done, to their mothers asking for new houses. Many NFL wives I've talked to expressed that their biggest financial challenge was their husbands' refusal to say no, especially to their moms, some of whom asked for new homes, new cars, vacations, and more. Other relatives asked for money to cover bills, investments, tuition, and just about everything. And the players felt bad even thinking about saying no. "How do I say no when my mom has helped me all along the way?" they'd ask.

THE 50-YARD LINE MOM

I don't think many rookie players have been told that it's ok to say no. It's my firm belief that not saying no is what gets a lot of these young men into trouble financially. They can't say no to their agent. They can't say no to their parent. And they can't say no to their friends.

Teach your son to say no. Assure him that he can be a caring person and still say no to family and friends. Let him know that it's okay to say no, even to you.

WHY I PARENT LIKE I DO

One reason I didn't have any financial expectations from my son's success is, in part, because I grew up extremely poor. My mother had four kids by the time she was 19 years old, and each was born only a year apart from the next. My family and I lived in a four-room shack in rural Kentucky with an outhouse and no running water for many years. We had to collect rain water in barrels in order to have water to bathe, and we drove to a gasoline station to fill gallon jugs and milk cans with water for drinking and cooking.

There were times that we didn't have any food in the house except for raisins. During the harsh winters, the icy wind blew right through our tin-roof home, and we would wake up to find our bed sheets covered with snow. I dreamed of living in the housing projects in my town because it had running water and indoor bathrooms. As a little girl,

THE NFL ROOKIE MOM

I thought you had arrived when you lived in the projects.

I started cleaning my teachers' houses when I was 10 years old so I could help my parents. I will never forget one lady in particular who lived in a great big white house that sat on a corner.

One day, I was working in her bathroom and she said, "Honey, get down on the floor and clean behind the toilet." At lunchtime, she made me sit out on the back porch to eat.

That experience was a great motivator because I felt there had to be a better life out there for me. I knew I had to do something different. I didn't exactly know what it was going to be at the time, but I knew that the Lord was going to see me through. I told myself, "I am not going to be cleaning floors on my hands and knees when I've got all this brainpower I can use."

My dad, who only had a fifth-grade education, thought going to college was absolutely ridiculous. He thought learning a trade was the sensible thing to do.

I didn't listen to my dad, nor to the school advisors who discouraged me from wanting to attend college. I started taking college classes when I was a senior in high school. I knew college was a way out for me. I thought, the more knowledge you have, the more control you have over your situation, and that is how you become successful.

There were only four black kids in my senior class at my high school where I was voted most likely to succeed and senior class president. I started to see the divine plan that God had for my life. I worked my way through college and graduated from nursing school, and then I went on to obtain a business degree.

I worked very hard to change my circumstances, but my parents never expected me to take care of them as I became successful. Instead, they complimented my accomplishments and were genuinely happy that I was able to make it on my own. Of course, if my parents needed anything, I would help them to the best of my ability.

I passed that same sentiment on to Jordan. I let him know that it's okay to say no, not just to friends and distant relatives, but to me and his dad as well. Once you start saying yes, it's difficult to stop.

I also instilled in him that he does not have to apologize for his success. He continues to work hard for it. I want him to be grateful for his blessings. He doesn't have to brag or flaunt his success, but he certainly shouldn't regret it. And more importantly, he shouldn't feel pressured to share it with anyone who asks him for money.

Mothers make the choice to bring their children into the world, not the other way around. If you want a piece of your child's financial pie, carve it out for yourself. Write a book, get an endorsement deal, produce a video, or give speeches. There are plenty of opportunities out there.

When our children are young, we owe them support, financial and otherwise. When they become successful, they don't owe us money, a mansion, or a Mercedes. And if you are lucky enough to get such a gift, it's likely because you raised a child who's grateful for your guidance, not one who feels he owes you.

THE LIFESTYLE

Many NFL Players Live Paycheck to Paycheck.[5]

PLAYING PRO BALL DOESN'T MEAN HE'S RICH

If your son makes it to the NFL, he will be paid well for a sport he loves to play. As a professional athlete, he should know how to manage his money, not squander it. Having a strong sense of financial responsibility is an important part of being a responsible adult. My children learned our three-step financial management strategy early on: give tithes to church, save a little bit, and then, if there was something that they wanted, they could spend.

The financial opportunity from playing in the NFL can give a young man a wonderful head start in life. Where else can you leave college at twenty-two or twenty-three years old and start out making

$320,000 or more per year? That was the base salary for the first year in the NFL when Jordan was a rookie. Everyone has the same base salary, but the signing bonus a player receives is based on the round in which he was drafted.

Even if your son plays only one year in the league, with careful financial management he can be so far ahead of many others who have been in the workforce for years. An important fact is that your son will always be a former NFL player, which is a title he can use to position himself well after leaving the league. There are many former players making a fortune who may have never played a down on the NFL field or who only played on the practice squad. I would tell Jordan all of the time, "Son, if you're smart, you will make more money off the field than you will ever make on the field. Keep that fact in mind." That is what I mean about financial opportunity.

CONTRACT MONEY VERSUS TAKE-HOME PAY

Some people think that if an athlete gets drafted and plays in the NFL, he is rich. To be honest, a yearly salary of $320,000 is a long way from being rich. Still, a common misconception is that all NFL players are rich. Many NFL rookies get caught up in that perception and try to live like a celebrity when they don't have the financial resources that celebrities have. So even if an athlete signs a multimillion-dollar contract, the money can disappear very quickly. Many

THE LIFESTYLE

athletes make the mistake of spending as if they'd received the full amount. They forget that a huge chunk goes to taxes and other expenses.

That mistake is the biggest financial downfall NFL rookies make, in my opinion.

To drive home my point about the difference between the contract money and what the NFL rookie actually brings home, here is an exercise we did with Jordan:

The first year, as you recall, NFL rookies were making $320,000. Uncle Sam would get his cut of about 33%; so that $320,000 salary gets cut by one-third, to $214,400.

We've always taught our kids to give back to the church off the top. Not the net, but the gross. For a $320,000 base salary, your tithes are $32,000. When you take $32,000 off for your tithes, you're now down to $182,400.

We also taught Jordan to save. So let's say you save 10% off the net, which is $18,240 that can be deposited into a 401k or a savings account. This leaves you with $164,160, which is the amount you will have to live on.

You're going to need a car. You have worked hard, so you'll want a nice car that you're going to enjoy. But remember, a car is just transportation, so don't overspend on a luxury car. Let's just say your car note is $1,000 a month. Multiply that by 12, and we will take $12,000 off your yearly salary for transportation, leaving you at $152,160.

Then you need shelter. You don't need to be

living in a penthouse. All that you need is a nice apartment. (Here, Jordan interjected, "OK, Mom and Dad, but I want to have two bedrooms so that when you all come for the games you will have a place to stay." A proud mom moment for me. We really appreciated his thoughtfulness.)

Consider that you might be working six months, so look for a six-month lease if that's available. Let's say you find a nice place for $2,500 a month. After you get the apartment, you have to pay for utilities, so that's probably another $200 a month. And for ease, you will just rent furniture, which is another $300 a month. You need to eat. So let's say $1,500 month. That totals $27,000 in basic living expenses for just six months.

Then there is entertainment. And you're going to need clothes, although you don't need designer clothes...

You start to see that there's a lot less money after taxes and expenses. You're talking about an amount that is *less than half* of the contract amount being the real amount of money you have to manage for the entire year. If you don't save some, live appropriately and within your means, and follow a budget, then it's very easy to see how you could create debt.

It would be very easy to end up in debt if you don't take a hard look at the real numbers.

That's why we suggested to Jordan that he needed to return home to Dallas after the season was over. In off-season, very few players stay in their

THE LIFESTYLE

team's city, unless it's already home. If he rented a place in Charlotte for the whole year, that would leave him paying rent for a place in Charlotte while staying with us in Dallas. If he chose to not stay at home and instead got his own place in Dallas, Jordan could have been paying rent on two different places. As a rookie player would that be a smart financial decision? We didn't think so. Needless to say, it was an eye-opening exercise for Jordan.

It's not difficult to see why many professional athletes get into financial trouble. The perceived flashy lifestyle of professional players often becomes a case of keeping up with the Joneses. Many of the highest-paid athletes also compete off the field, buying new cars, big houses, jewelry, and so on, but the reality is much different for other players. For those at the bottom of the earning ranks, money can be tight, and many live paycheck to paycheck.

I think that when your son is faced with people who want money from him, it helps to crunch the numbers. When an NFL rookie sits down and does this financial assessment, he can see in black and white exactly how much money he has left over. Knowing what he really has in the bank makes it easy to say no. Well, let me say it like this, it makes it *easier* to say no.

This exercise really made Jordan think. And even though he didn't like it, he finally agreed with us and realized it was wiser to stay home following his rookie season.

MY ADVICE ON FINANCIAL INVESTING

First, a disclaimer: I am not a financial professional, but I do have firsthand experience with the financial choices your son may face on his journey to and through professional sports. At the Rookie Symposium, financial managers speak to the players about investing their money. My view on investing would be controversial in most financial circles, but here it is: I think most rookie players do not need to invest in anything.

As demonstrated in the earlier exercise, rookie players take home much less than their contract pay once all of their expenses are deducted. For the first year, it's all about having cash, in my opinion. These rookie players need to save and have cash on hand. Your son should think about investing when he has extra money, when possibly losing that investment would be less of a concern.

Investments are always a risk. Yes, there can be great rewards, but the stock market can be extremely volatile.

Let's say your son invested $60,000 of his first year's salary. If he gets cut, he'd have that much less to pay his rent, car payment, and all his bills until he gets another job or until another team calls him back. Please don't let your son get caught up in the false thinking that he has hundreds of thousands of dollars to invest at this stage of his career. He doesn't really have enough cash to invest in anything yet.

THE LIFESTYLE

ROOKIE LIVING ARRANGEMENTS

In his first year, Jordan was drafted and received a bonus with the draft. So coming right out of college, he was making quite a bit of money. He wasn't a top-round draft pick, but it doesn't matter. As a rookie player, he was still making more money than I was making at the time.

As mentioned, there was no reason to spend money on two places to live, because he was only in Charlotte for five or six months, and then he'd be back home in Dallas. Again, he didn't like the idea when we first proposed it, but by the end of his first season he had saved quite a bit of money. While he was living at home, the goal was to focus on putting money back into savings. During his second year, it made more sense for him to get his own place.

Because Jordan lived at home during his first year, he was able to save enough money to put a deposit down on his own place. This way, he could own something. During his second season in the league, he had an apartment in Charlotte, but he put a large down payment on a home here in Dallas, a home that was located close to us, so my husband and I could watch the place while Jordan was gone for the season.

We told Jordan that he needed to use his money to pay off his mortgage as soon as he could. If Jordan wanted to spend money on toys, we advised him to wait and use his bonus money to pay for them. His salary was needed for living expenses, we explained. Thankfully, he listened to us.

To illustrate this point, we took it a step further by asking him, "Tell us what you would do if you weren't playing football? What type of job would you have? What would you do? And what type of income would that bring you? Based on that income, you can determine the type of home to buy and your budget for living."

Jordan thought about those questions, and in two-and-half years, he paid off the mortgage on his house.

I believe you have to start very early teaching your son about financial responsibility. You've got to get him in the habit of understanding—even if it's just a nickel here or a dime there—that there are three principles to finance: give, save, then spend. If your son will live his life by those three principles, then he will probably be financially sound.

LIVE WHERE IT MAKES THE MOST SENSE

There is so much uncertainty during that rookie year and throughout your son's time in the NFL. Your son may not know where he is going to be from season to season, so he needs to feel pretty comfortable about where he ultimately wants to live. That's why I would encourage a young player in the league to slow down. It may sound good for him to buy a house as soon as he joins the league, but the timing has to be right, and it has to make financial sense. Jordan knew he wanted to come back and live in

THE LIFESTYLE

Dallas. Purchasing a home is a huge investment, so it was important for him to find a place where his money would grow.

Originally, Jordan wanted to buy a big house in a suburb of Dallas. I said to him, "Son, look at the growth in that area. There's no growth. If you buy a house, it will require yard work and other maintenance, and you aren't here. Get yourself a townhouse, something a bachelor would live in. It needs to be located in a vibrant area where it would be easy to sell or to rent if you need it to become rental property. Get something you can afford even if you're not playing ball."

Jordan took my advice and bought a townhouse in an urban mixed-use area in far North Dallas. It was one of the best financial moves he's ever made. Jordan's home increased in value in four years. Real estate agents were calling him, wanting him to sell his place. I said to him, "Do you understand that when you sell your townhouse, that's clear money for you? You won't have a mortgage you have to pay off and the house will have appreciated in value. You listened and bought a place where there was a lot of growth—in an area people are moving to and a place where people want to live. It was a great investment for you."

I think in order to position himself well for home ownership, a rookie player should consider having a roommate or be very conservative with his finances that first year in the league. I'm talking about most of the players, not the ones who have multimillion-dollar contracts. If your son has the chance to get a roommate, then he should do so to save as much money as possible. When he is ready to buy a place, your son can make a sizable down payment. The down payment brings down the mortgage, and having a manageable mortgage will really help him going forward.

Even if he had continued to play for several more years, Jordan realized that he really didn't need a huge place because he would seldom be there. And since he would be gone for the season, his dad and I would be the ones taking care of his property. If we didn't, then he would have to hire a property management company to watch it and manage it. So that's even more money going out of his pocket.

In their second year, NFL players were making about $420,000. Ideally, your son would have saved money that first year. Now he has received a $100,000 raise. The third year, the players would make about $530,000. In my opinion, this is a good time to start thinking about buying a house—after salary increases of nearly $100,000 per year for the second and third years in the league.

My advice for those rookie NFL players who do buy a home during their second year: Find one that's reasonable—one that you can afford. Then try to pay it off during your third year. That way, you'll always have somewhere to live. That's what you need. It doesn't have to be a mansion. But you will leave the NFL with somewhere to live that's already bought and paid for.

THE LIFESTYLE

Having a home that's paid off is an incredible head start in life for a young man in his early twenties. It affords him the opportunity to be flexible. If he decides he wants to be an entrepreneur, he's not tied down to a mortgage. He's able to live a dream at an incredibly young age. Jordan and his wife had a great start for their marriage because they are homeowners and don't have a mortgage. As his parents, we had to learn all these financial lessons on our own.

Of course, now Jordan struts around proudly telling people how he saved up his money, bought a house, and paid for his home in two years. Could it be that his financial success was a result of listening to his parents? It makes me laugh. I tell Jordan often, "You know, your parents do know a little something."

Tell your son to listen to people who know something. It doesn't have to be his mom and dad, but tell him not to listen to his buddies, especially if they don't have any more than your son does. Many of his friends will probably have much less.

CREDIT CARDS ARE NOT A NECESSITY

The other thing we shared with Jordan was to avoid debt. As young people, my husband and I weren't given that message, so we found ourselves having to get out of debt. Typically, you leave college and you're in debt, and then you get in more debt by just living life. We didn't want Jordan to experience

THE 50-YARD LINE MOM

that financial burden, especially since the NFL gave him the opportunity to live life differently and to be debt-free.

As a professional athlete, your son will get many credit card offers. Jordan would say, "Mom, all my friends say you have to have a credit card."

"Why?" I would ask. "If you have cash, people will take cash! You don't need credit cards. Trust me. They will take cash."

"I know, but you need credit cards to live," Jordan said.

But thankfully, once again, he listened to our advice. Jordan did not have a credit card for the five years that I managed his NFL career. I said, "Jordan, if you can't pay cash for it, then you don't need it. If you've got a debit card, you've got something to hold a hotel room and do all of those things, but the money that is being spent is money that you actually have. And it will help you manage your finances better."

So Jordan wasn't in any credit card debt when he left the league. I can't say you can guide every child that way because there are some who are not going to listen. You can raise five kids in the same home and you are going to have five different minds. But Jordan was obedient and he listened to our wise counsel. Because of that, even after football, he's okay financially. From the beginning of his professional football career, he lived a manageable lifestyle—one that he could maintain once he no longer played in the NFL.

THE LIFESTYLE

TRANSPORTATION

In college, Jordan drove an old, beat-up truck that we bought for him. During his senior year, we told Jordan that we would buy him a car since we really didn't have to pay for his education. In reality, it was the most expensive "free" education I've ever seen. Holy smoke! We spent a lot of money on travel, hotel, and lodging to watch him play football all over the country, never missing one of his games. He said, "No, I want to earn the new car that I get, so I want to buy it myself."

When Jordan was ready to buy his first car, we told him that he should reward himself, since he worked so hard. We tried to guide him in our own way. My husband was really good at that.

"Do you really need a $100,000 car? Or will a $40,000 car get you where you need to go?" Chuck asked him. "Save your money, and reward yourself each step of the way. Maybe use money from your signing bonus to get yourself a car. Of course, you don't want to use all of your signing bonus for a car."

So instead of buying a $100,000 luxury car, Jordan bought himself an affordable SUV. Some of his friends didn't understand it.

"Man, this is what you're getting? I thought you would be getting a Mercedes."

Jordan would tell them the SUV was all he needed. We reminded him that he also had to pay the cost of transporting that vehicle back and forth to Charlotte.

THE 50-YARD LINE MOM

My husband went with Jordan to the dealership to help him negotiate a good deal on his new car. We'd heard and read stories of young men being taken advantage of all the time, including a few of Jordan's teammates. The salespeople saw these young rookie players coming. One teammate wanted a beautiful little Mustang, and the dealership told him he didn't have any credit and that he was high risk. So they charged him 20% interest on the auto loan. TWENTY PERCENT!

At the negotiating table, Jordan's dad said, "It's true my son doesn't have credit. He doesn't need credit because he can pay cash. Is he going to pay cash for a truck? No! That makes no sense."

You don't pay cash for a depreciating asset. As a result of Chuck's negotiating skills, Jordan walked out of the dealership that day with a good deal on the vehicle he wanted with no interest.

Encourage your son to take someone with him to the negotiating table who is knowledgeable and really has his best interest at heart. Of course, your son has to be willing to listen and follow good advice. But again, that starts very early on. You have to bring your kids up thinking about things in a way that has them saying to themselves, *"Here goes Mom and Dad again. I guess I'd better listen."*

There was one player who was really good with the concept of driving only what you need and can afford. He was a very popular young man who played with Jordan on the Washington Redskins.

THE LIFESTYLE

Jordan was in his second year with the Redskins when they met.

The young man was a sixth-round draft pick. And when you're a sixth-round draft pick, you're unfortunately perceived as being *only a sixth-round draft pick.*

But, he got his break. Someone got injured, and this player came in and ended up being the starter for two years. So he was very, very fortunate and got a few television spots and endorsement deals.

But remember, whether you're a sixth-round draft pick or drafted in the first round, your salary was still $320,000 a year. That kid drove around in an old, beat-up car for two years. He said, "This car gets me around. I know that this is not long term, but I've got transportation."

Everyone laughed at him. They'd ask, "Why are you driving around in that old, beat-up car? You're an NFL player." I'm sure that this young man has a new car now because he worked hard for it. He understood the concept of not overspending just because he was playing in the league. When Jordan got his new SUV, to him it was wonderful. Compared to the old, beat-up truck he'd been driving, Jordan probably felt like he was driving a Rolls Royce.

As I mentioned, Jordan put a down payment on his house during his second year in the league. But we advised him to wait until the end of the season to make any other big purchases.

THE 50-YARD LINE MOM

If you want a toy, go down and score a touchdown; it's in your contract. Or a certain number of tackles; it's in your contract. At the end of the season, you'll get that extra bonus. It's money outside of your budget, so use that to buy a toy. If you get a bonus, then treat yourself. But even then, don't spend all of your bonus.

Over the course of his career, Jordan ended up getting some pretty nice toys. At the end of his second season, he used his bonus to purchase a Jaguar. That was his treat.

In his third year, Jordan paid off his house. Then, going into his fourth year, he decided that he really wanted a two-seater Mercedes. My husband asked him, "How many cars can you drive at once? You've got an SUV that you ship back and forth. Now you have a Jaguar that sits in the garage while you're playing during the season. So what do you need a Mercedes for?"

Jordan wasn't really interested in hearing that advice. He kept saying, "I really want this two-seater Mercedes. I really want it." We didn't tell him no, don't buy it, but we did tell him to think about it.

My husband always told Jordan to think about big decisions. In this case, Chuck posed these questions to him: "How many cars can you drive at once? What's wrong with the Jaguar that now you need a Mercedes? And don't you think you're being a little bit greedy? You're making good money, but you're not a multimillionaire."

Thank goodness Jordan didn't buy it. Because then he would have had an extra car payment going

THE LIFESTYLE

into his fifth year in the league, and that's when he got cut.

The point here is this: Don't spend money you don't have yet.

Jordan still wants to buy that two-seater Mercedes. It's just going to take him longer to get it. He's going to have to do it a different way. But he still has a beautiful Jaguar and his SUV sitting in the garage. We told him to invest his money in things that appreciate, not in items like cars that depreciate.

We gave Jordan another piece of advice about cars and finances. He wanted to pay off his SUV. We didn't agree. "Why do you want to do that? You have a zero-interest rate. Why would you want to tie up $40,000 of cash, liquid money, to pay off a depreciating asset?"

Jordan hadn't thought about it that way. "It's not costing you anything to make monthly payments. The only thing it's costing you is a stamp and writing a check." (Even less these days with automatic drafts directly from your bank account.)

So why did we advise against paying off his car? It's really about balance. In the worst case scenario, if disaster strikes, then sell the car. At least he would still have that $40,000 in the bank that he can live off of for food and essentials. He could take a bus if he had to, but he would still have money in the bank to live on.

That's the way your son needs to start thinking—financially smart.

While it's important that we approached financial budgeting with a well thought-out plan, having these conversations long before draft day helped establish a solid foundation. It's never too late to start talking about smart financial planning. Mothers are the centers of many athletes' lives, and encouraging them to pave the path toward a secure financial future is one of the most important influences we can have.

DRUGS, ALCOHOL, AND PARTYING

I'd tell any mother's son the same thing I told Jordan: Just say no to drugs, alcohol, and excessive partying. Stay away from that and don't do it. My husband phrased his advice a bit differently. Chuck told Jordan to "keep his head on a swivel." What he meant was for Jordan to constantly be looking around so he could avoid bad influences, bad situations, and bad people. My husband would say, "Don't be in a situation where you're not doing anything wrong but you're guilty by association because of the people you're with or the situation you're in."

Of course, a rookie NFL player needs to understand what drugs and alcohol can do to his budding career. The advice I gave my son was primarily about their effects on his health. "Jordan, you can't run up and down the field all day long in the heat, two or three times a day, and be hung over without it eventually taking a toll on your body. If your body is your product, then you really have to look at what you're putting into it."

THE LIFESTYLE

Whether it was steroids, painkillers, or illegal drugs, I tried to give Jordan advice from a medical perspective. Almost all medication, whether over-the-counter, prescription, or illegal, has a side effect. Eventually, the drug messes with your body.

"I can't stop you from doing it," I'd tell him, "but if you do decide to take drugs of any kind, just be educated enough to know what the consequences are."

In regard to excessive partying and drinking, it's the same thing. "How do you think you're gonna stay out all night and expect to perform out on the field the next day? You can do that when you're 22 or 23 years old, but I assume you want to stay in the league a long time. If you keep partying into your late 20s, it's going to catch up with you. Plus, if you're out partying, nine times out of ten, it's not a controlled environment. Something bad is probably going to happen."

As my husband likes to say, "Nothing good happens after midnight."

One time, Jordan was out in Las Vegas and there was a photo taken of him with a glass in his hand. The picture suggested that he was a party animal who was chugging booze. When I talked to him about it, he said, "Mom, it was just a glass of soda."

"I don't know that," I said. "It looks like a mixed drink. It's okay if you were drinking because you are of age, but just know that's the perception. You just need to be mindful of that."

I wasn't trying to make Jordan paranoid, but there are cameras everywhere. There are cameras on walls, in elevators, on street corners, and in just about every single person's hand these days because everyone has a cell phone! Remind your son that everything he does could be recorded. It's best to avoid questionable situations, even if he isn't doing anything wrong, because someone's going to take a picture.

THE OVERNIGHT CELEBRITY

"The experience of being famous is something for which no one is prepared."[6]

YOUR SON'S PUBLIC IMAGE

One of the first things I asked Jordan when he became an NFL player was, "What do you want your image to be? Do you want to be that hip-hop, chain-wearing type? Is that the image that you want to portray? Or do you want to be perceived as a professional?" My advice to him from the beginning has always been that you have to think about life after football. What do you want to be? And based on the image you want to create, that's the way you interact with people.

So what is that image going to be? Where are your opportunities? Jordan graduated from Texas

THE 50-YARD LINE MOM

A&M University, which has one of the best alumni networks in the country. Many people may have stereotypes about athletes, so he's going to have to overcome that stereotype from the beginning. "How you present yourself, how you speak, and how you look are going to determine what opportunities you're going to get," I'd tell him.

For those players who are flashy, everything is wonderful until they're no longer in the league. Then what are they going to do? It's easier to have an image that you are proud of from the start than to try to reinvent yourself later on.

Whenever we could, we tried to tell Jordan to be careful of social media. "Son, don't post anything that you don't want to be out there for the rest of your life. You don't have to respond to everything."

If you are going to respond, keep it brief. Just say yes or no. Don't offer a lot of opinions. Keep it casual. Be careful who you invite into your network. Because it may not be you posting, but there's a reflection of you that gets out on your Facebook timeline, your Twitter feed, your Instagram posts, your Snapchat stories, and other social media that projects who you are. What appears on your page or in your feed reflects back on you, even if you didn't post it yourself.

Your presence on social media, the people you're hanging around, the way you live your life... all of it matters.

I'd tell him, "As long as I'm your manager, you're not going to be perceived as a party animal because

THE OVERNIGHT CELEBRITY

you're going to be thinking about life after football. So think about that."

I'll tell you, now that I've gotten older, there are things that Jordan posts that I don't like, but I'm old-school. I know you have to be with the times, but I still think, *"Son, you probably shouldn't go there, but you're not asking me now. I got you through those first five years, so now you're on your own."*

BEING IN THE PUBLIC EYE

It's a privilege to be an NFL player in the public eye. There's going to come a time when no one is going to ask for your son's autograph. And you also never know who you are encountering. Be polite. Say hello, shake a hand, and then move on. You don't have to truly engage with them, but just be polite. Rely on your gut feelings about people. That will help you recognize the people that you need to stay clear of.

The thing that's always been said about Jordan is that he is a really, really nice guy and well-mannered. One time, he went to the doctor in maybe his third year in the NFL. That physician later told me he couldn't believe that Jordan was an NFL player. When I asked him why, the doctor said, "Because he's so nice. Most of the players that come in here act like they own the place, that they've got priority. They are sometimes rude, but your son was humble."

That's the greatest compliment I could ever have as a mom because that's how we raised him to be. Good manners and a great reputation will carry your son a long way because he will be remembered long after he has finished playing professional football.

THE MEDIA SPOTLIGHT

I have tried to paint an accurate picture of our journey through the NFL with positive intent, even when it doesn't always sound positive. The opportunity and the the experience of playing professional football is *un-believ-able!* I mean, it's just *wonderful!* But you have to learn to manage the media scrutiny and focus on the big picture. Remember that, as with any job, you don't know what it's *really* like until you get there.

My passion is to help rookie players, their parents, and significant others enjoy the NFL experience and navigate their way through it with helpful information, wisdom, and advice from our own experiences. Had I known what being in the league was *really* going to be like, I could have been better prepared.

You have to have incredibly thick skin. I haven't had the experience that moms of high-profile players have, but I can only imagine how hurtful it must be to hear the media or the fans browbeat your son— hourly, daily, at times, for weeks on end. Things are reported that you know are not true. It leads you to want to react, but sometimes you can't, and in most cases, you *shouldn't.* Your role at this stage of his life is to nurture, support, and calm your son. False reports make you want to set the record straight. But it's not for you to do, because your son is a grown man now.

THE OVERNIGHT CELEBRITY

GROUPIES, BAD FRIENDS, BAD INFLUENCES

If I could give other moms one piece of advice, it would be to become very visible in your son's life. Present yourself in such a way that others know you are always around and watching. I think it's the best deterrent to keep groupies, bad friends, and bad influences away.

When your son becomes a professional athlete, the women, or groupies, come out of the woodwork. It's unbelievable.

I was quick to say, "Oh no. Who is this? Where did she come from? No, we are not having that."

You may need to step in to close ranks and protect your son's inner circle of friends and associates. You may have to say "no" to groupie women hanging around and shoo them away. You need to feel comfortable doing that. The comfort level you feel to intervene on your son's behalf is directly related to the relationship you have built with your son from the very beginning of his football career, and it continues to evolve after he enters the league.

Here are the questions a mom might ask a rookie NFL player about the women entering his life after he's in the league:

"Yes, you want to find someone that looks good, but does she always have her makeup on? Do you never really get to see the true person?"

"Does she work? Does she have a job? Does she have a meaningful job? Are you two on similar levels?

"You're college-educated. Is she college-educated? It

THE 50-YARD LINE MOM

doesn't mean that she has to have graduated from college, but is she aspiring to be something?"

"Can she live without you? Does she have her own money? Does she have a good work ethic? Is she someone who can contribute and not just take?"

I think either the mother or a significant woman in the player's life, whether it's the grandmother, the aunt, or the lady down the street, really shows a young player what to look for in women and will help keep the gold-diggers away. The father figure, on the other hand, shows him what to look for in his friends.

"Does he have a job? Is it a meaningful job? Or is he in the club every night trying to look for women?"

Chuck and I were intentional about the things that we would say to our children. Many people assume children automatically absorb the values and ideas your family holds dear. They may not realize that they actually have to articulate their ideals and verbally communicate the wisdom they want to share and pour into their children.

I advised Jordan to find someone who was going to encourage him, and that deep encouragement was what he should be looking for. I think we all raise intelligent kids. I'm not going to say Jordan is a genius, or my daughter, Dominique, is a genius. But most kids have intuition, and they need to learn to trust it.

So tell your son, "You're not looking for the person who always says that you're wonderful and that you're right all the time. You're looking for the person who will tell you what they really think in a respectful way. It's that person who becomes like a second set of eyes for you. She will step in as your partner to watch over you like we did as your parents. She should be looking out for your best interests. Someone who sees something in you that you don't see in yourself. You want to find the person who is pulling stuff out of you that you didn't know you had. I think that's what a significant other does for you. She is someone who really has your best interests at heart."

Be cautious of the flashy persona and lifestyle of some women who hover around professional athletes. Advise your son to put up his protective shield if all he sees her wearing are designer labels, and the woman works a minimum-wage job. You know what I'm saying? That's just a common sense thing.

Think about how that woman is able to dress like that…or why. If she doesn't have a job that supports that lifestyle, she may have a lot of debt.

Both my husband and I explained to Jordan how important it was that he be aware of the financial situation of anyone he might consider marrying. If the woman he was interested in marrying had debt, we told him, the two of them needed to figure out, *before* the wedding, how that debt was going to be paid.

"You don't come with a lot of debt, so don't bring someone else into your life who does," I told him. "If this woman has to have Louis Vuitton, and you see

THE 50-YARD LINE MOM

more than two or three designer bags in her closet, much of your money is probably going to be spent maintaining that lifestyle for her. She's high maintenance. Avoid a woman who's high maintenance."

I remember telling Jordan when he was twenty-six, "You own a home. Most 26-year olds don't own a home. Find a woman who is working and saving so that she can have her own home. You need to find someone with compatible goals."

I used the home ownership example a lot. I talked a lot about how a woman dresses, especially if she's usually in designer goods from head to toe. I talked about finding a woman that's pulling out the best in him. Maybe she says something like, "You had a great play on the field, but I love the way you interacted with the young fans after the game, encouraging them like a mentor. That could be the source of a future career opportunity for you."

Meet her family and meet her mother. You will learn a lot about the woman by observing her mom. For the most part, a girl will follow the pattern of her mother, but of course, there are exceptions.

So my advice is to meet the parents, and *then* assess the young lady. Because if, for example, she grew up in a house where the father abused the mother every other week, and the mom stayed, that's probably all she knows. So when she finds a man that's really going to treat her well, she may not know how to receive it.

It's that kind of advice that helps your children. But the biggest deterrent to negative influences is every time they turn around, they see the mama and the daddy there.

For the record, the worst influences of all can be the businessmen who are always trying to cut a deal and the disreputable agents out there. I define a bad influence as anyone who is after your son for something that may not be in his best interest. So the bad element around a young player isn't always his friends or the scores of beautiful women with questionable intentions. It could also include those people in a position of power who also want something from your son. There are many people who will target someone who is a little bit vulnerable, especially if he doesn't have good people around him watching, advising, and protecting him.

NOTHING IS REALLY FREE

Your son's life is completely different as a professional athlete. It's not like college anymore. In college, no one can give your son money, and no one can do things for him. There are NCAA rules in place that protect the players. In the pros, your son may have an agent in his ear constantly telling him what he should do. With draft prospects and rookies, many agents try hard to elevate the player's ego and seduce him with offers. "Let me take you out to dinner… let me manage this and let me do that." For some young men, it may feel good to say, "Call my agent" or "Call my people." That's an ego thing. Rookie players can get caught up in that.

THE 50-YARD LINE MOM

Agents get caught up in being "the man" for their clients as well.

I have always told Jordan that there is no such thing as getting something for free. There's always a cost. As an NFL player, Jordan would walk into any restaurant and get stopped for his autographs and pictures. Many times his meal was on the house. It's easy to get caught up in all of that. He may have received dinner for free, but there were costs associated with that "free" meal. In most cases, your son may not have an issue paying the cost if it's an autograph or having his picture on the restaurant's wall. But don't ever allow your son to believe someone is giving him something for nothing. Nothing is given free and clear with no strings attached. There's nothing wrong with accepting a free dinner, but understand there's a cost or sacrifice associated with accepting it or any other freebie.

NFL GAME DAY

Psychologists link family traditions with higher academic success, happiness, and emotional well-being.[7]

SEEING JORDAN ON FIELD FOR THE FIRST TIME

The very first time I saw Jordan on the field as an NFL player was in Charlotte, North Carolina. It was a beautiful fall day, and there was not a cloud in the sky. Panther Stadium was a sea of iconic Carolina blue. It was a preseason game, and my sister and her daughter were with me. I remember that our seats were very high up. I was sitting at the end zone, wearing a team jersey with Jordan's name and number, and waiting for Jordan to come out of the tunnel.

They typically announce the players who start

as they walk out. Every other game, they alternate between offense and defense starting the game. For this particular game, the Panthers defense was on the field first and Jordan was starting. When they announced Jordan's name, his picture was projected up on the jumbotron. It said: **"Jordan Pugh, Texas A&M University."**

Watching him run out of the tunnel at the start of his first professional football game was amazing. It was the first time I saw him in the Carolina Panthers uniform. My sister and I were so overwhelmed with emotion that our eyes welled with tears of pride. I started thinking about all of those years that brought us to that point. I thought about the first time Jordan announced that he was going to be an NFL player someday. I thought about my skepticism about it ever becoming a reality. I thought about the time he broke his arm in the 8th grade and still wanted to play, which made me a nervous wreck. I thought about all the ups and downs when he was in college. All those memories, milestones, joys, and pains that had brought us to this moment.

It was a very emotional time, but I also felt a tremendous sense of gratitude. Who was I to be sitting in the stands at an NFL game? Typically, I would be watching a pro game on television, and now my son was part of it. The feeling of watching my son follow his passion and fulfill his lifelong dream—and being part of that journey with him—was just unbelievable. To be there at the stadium for his first NFL start is a memory I will never forget.

NFL GAME DAY

NAVIGATING THROUGH THE BALL CLUB

Playing in the NFL is a once-in-a-lifetime opportunity, and you never know how long it's going to last. So from day one, think about what your son is going to do off the field and network with everyone who crosses your path. Building a strong network was my focus from the day Jordan got drafted.

What I have learned over the years is to contact the team's front-office organization and introduce yourself as a player's mom. Speak with someone in their public relations department and tell them that you want to be engaged. Ask them how to do that. There is typically a wives group and sometimes a moms group in place that you can join.

I contacted the Carolina Panthers office during the preseason and introduced myself as a mother who wanted to be involved and who wanted to help the organization. Were there any mother's organizations I could join? Were there any community activities with the Panthers that I could be involved in? One thing that I did when I was in town, or at Panthers Stadium, was go to the front office to meet with the PR person, with whom I'd already spoken on the phone. They're usually around for the games. At that point, it was only a matter of introducing myself. Once you make yourself visible, you find that they get to know you, and they start calling you to get connected and engaged.

My advice: Take the time to find out how you can connect to the team in a more personal way. You

THE 50-YARD LINE MOM

will become known to the organization as that mom who really wants to be involved. It's always about helping the organization, and you will find yourself in positions and meeting people you never thought you would be able to meet—like the team owners, the president of the organization, and the coaches. It can be kind of intimidating, but all you have to do is say "hi." You never know where the conversation might lead.

My husband and I got in good with the press because we were often the only parents there when the team traveled. So the cameramen would start coming up to us to ask us how we were doing. Then, because the president of the Panthers was always there, he started waving at us when he saw us.

Once, after a game in Seattle, we saw the president of the Panthers standing alone. No one would go over to talk to him, but I did. I walked over and said, "Hello, my name is Jo Ann Pugh, Jordan Pugh's mom." We started talking, and he found out about Dominique and learned more about Jordan. I would venture to say that I may be one of the only parents who has ever done that. It's something so unusual that this man has remembered me and now there's a connection.

Whenever I traveled to Charlotte, I would send him a little note: "In Charlotte, looking at Panther Stadium, hope you are well." Two minutes later I'd get a response from him, "Great hearing from you." Even when Jordan was released from Carolina, I sent a very nice email that said, "I am really sorry to see that my son has been cut. I understand, but I want to thank you for the last two years."

He sent me a note back: "I knew you all were a classy family. I wish him nothing but the best."

Every year since, I've kept in contact with him. I've never asked him for anything—it's just been about the relationship. Is there value in that? Absolutely. I think that one of the shortcomings of young men and women today is that they don't value that human interaction. They don't value the building of a network. If you want to succeed, you've got to have a network. Social media alone is a not a replacement for one-on-one human interaction.

We also developed a little network with the parents of other players, but the challenge is that you are constantly meeting a new group of folks because the players change so often. We were constantly engaging with new people, but the benefit is that it expands your network.

If you're a parent, connect with the wives. It is surprising how many of these young women really need some mentoring. I told you about one of the wives telling me that her greatest challenge with her husband was getting him to say no. Sometimes the wives just want someone to talk to about this experience, particularly those who really understand that this is a short-term opportunity to be maximized.

Then there are some moms who are not that much older than their sons. If you happen to be that younger parent, seek out the older women who have sons who have been in the league for a while and ask questions. "Tell me what you've done? Tell me how you navigated this? How did you help your child to get through it? How did you deal with constantly moving, helping your child through that?"

Most parents don't know about the NFL Players Association (NFLPA). It's headquartered in Washington, D.C., and works on behalf of the players. If you want to visit, all you have to do is call and let them know. During one trip to Washington, I spent half a day touring the NFLPA office. I met with the NFLPA president who negotiates all the players' contracts. I sat down with him for an hour and asked him what I needed to know as a parent in the NFL. There is also a mothers' organization that you can join—the Professional Football Players Mothers Association. Your agent should be able to provide you with a lot of useful information as well.

Know what your goals are, and focus on getting helpful information that you can provide to your son. I tried to educate Jordan with the information I gathered from the NFLPA and his agent. *"Do you know that your contract says this?"* Most players don't read their contracts. *"Do you know that you have this benefit? Do you know that you can go to the NFLPA and they have these resources for you?"*

Connecting with the organization on all levels, being involved with the community, and recognizing that the NFL experience is not going to last very long are the best ways to navigate through the professional ball club. It's important to maximize the unique opportunity that professional football provides.

GAME DAY TRADITIONS

From college to the pros, our family did two things as part of our Game Day traditions. If Jordan was able to meet us the night before the game, we would have dinner together. We would just let him talk about the upcoming game. We would often see the coaches, the team owners, and other players. Some of the guys would come up and say, "Boy, you know, I wish my mom or dad was here." We'd always invite them to sit down and join us.

The other tradition we had is that we always made our way down to the field. It got to the point that everyone on the team knew that the Pughs were going to be down on the sidelines. We prayed together as a family before Jordan went into the locker room before kickoff. I didn't care if people liked seeing us pray or not. I knew that my son needed protection over him for that game, so we would pray. After the game, we'd watch Jordan get on the bus, and then we'd head back home ourselves.

GAME DAY LOGISTICS

Seating at the games for family and friends of the players was actually very exciting. In college, the player got four free tickets. But in the pros, the player has to pay for the seats. The player typically gets two tickets. So when family members ask their NFL player to get tickets for them and their friends, it's coming out of the player's pocket.

At the home stadium, players can usually get fairly decent seats. The exact location of the seats varies by team. You won't be sitting on the 50-yard line, but the seats are typically in a decent location.

Seating at away games is a different matter altogether. Seat availability is limited to what the away team releases for the visiting team, and it's usually in the nosebleed section. The family member has to "buy up" to get better seats in a different section.

Once, when we were in Arizona, one of Jordan's teammates had about 25 family members at the game. (That's when the concept of "it's hard to say no" comes back into play.) He was a sixth- or seventh-round draft pick, so he wasn't making a whole lot of money, and those game tickets are very expensive. It can cost between $85 to $100 each to purchase seats in the "nosebleed" section. For away games, the ticket prices are sometimes even more expensive.

In Charlotte, there was an area right outside of the locker room where all of the family could meet up with the players after the game. In Washington, we were seated in the club level. There was a designated family section with pretty decent seats and a little bit better access to the locker room. At the end of the game, we could walk right out of the club and get to the locker room fairly easily.

NFL GAME DAY

I was surprised by some of the hotels the teams stayed in during away games. They were very modest and each player had a roommate. I was thinking, *"These are NFL players and they're staying here?"* It was often difficult to find out where the players were going to stay the night before the game or what the player rate was so that the family could stay at the hotel too. Some teams, though, had their players stay at hotels like the Four Seasons. It's really up to the owner and the amount they want to spend on hotel accommodations. Some teams allow family members to access their hotel rate. It never hurts to ask.

BEFORE THE GAME

For away games, the team arrives the day before the game. Ask your player relations person for their team's travel itinerary. It will tell you what time they arrive at the hotel the day before the game. Players usually have team meetings until about 6 p.m. Then it's free time for the players for about three hours, or until their curfew before the next meeting.
We'd meet Jordan during his free time and have dinner together as a family. It was an opportunity for him to talk to us about anything he chose, whether it was something that was bothering him or the upcoming game. Sometimes it was just casual conversation to calm down before a game. Then we would walk back to the hotel and just sit around in the hotel lobby and talk.

THE 50-YARD LINE MOM

There would be other players who would come by, and they would talk with us as well. Some of the coaches would come by and see us there, which gave us all the opportunity to get to know each other. Sometimes it would be the team owners, which allowed the owners to get to know us too. We would leave when it was time for Jordan to go to his final meeting. If we were staying at that same hotel, we would go to our room. If it was a home game, we would go back to his apartment to stay.

Make sure you get to the game site at least two hours prior to the start time. It gives you ample time to find parking and get comfortable without having to rush. You're already there, so you have an opportunity to see your son before he goes into the locker room. Sometimes a player gets hurt during warm-ups and the coaches need to get in touch with the family. Or you just might want to see what's going on with your son with your own eyes. It's so much easier to do if you're already at the stadium. So just plan to get there early. Sit back, relax, and take it all in. That is my advice to any player mom, but especially those of you who have never attended a professional football game in person.

Over time, we learned to navigate our way around the stadium a bit. We figured out how to get down on the sidelines, and it was simply by asking, since we were the parents of a player. Some teams are more receptive and helpful than others. We were able to do this in Charlotte. Every game we would

NFL GAME DAY

say, "We are Jordan Pugh's parents, and we want to stand on the sidelines for pregame warm-up."

The people working in the stadium were very gracious in allowing us that limited access. We would go down and watch Jordan and the team warm up before they went back into the locker room to dress out. Then they would come out for pregame drills prior to going back into the locker room a second time before the game started.

A lot of parents would ask us, "How do you get down on the sidelines? I would love to be down there for pregame warm-up." The best thing you can do is just call the team office and ask for either player relations or the public relations department. Just identify yourself as the parent of a player and express your interest in being on the sidelines during pregame warm-up. If they approve your request, they will provide you with sideline passes. We were fortunate because we never had anyone tell us no.

No matter where he was on the field, Jordan would always run over to meet us on the sideline and we would pray together. We didn't ask Jordan to do this. Jordan took the initiative to come over to us for our family prayer. He would say, "Come on, Mom, Dad, let's pray."

We would pray for protection and pray for the team, and then watch Jordan go into the locker room. It became one of our most cherished pre-game traditions. We'd hear comments from some of the people in the stands that it was just a beautiful thing to see. But we weren't doing it for show. We did it as an expression of our faith. Sometimes you have an opportunity to reach people you never thought you'd reach.

DURING AND AFTER THE GAME

After the warm-up, we'd watch the game. And by "watch the game," I mean I would watch the offense play. Remember, Jordan played defense. I *couldn't* watch when Jordan was on the field. I would go to the bathroom. Chuck would say, "I know you went to every game, but I don't know how much of the game you saw."

I would just wait for the instant replays so I could see what happened, then I could tell Jordan later that he did a great job. I didn't want to see him get hurt, and I didn't want to see him get hit. I needed those few seconds of tape delay. I wanted to make sure that he was okay, and when I would see Jordan get up after a play, then I was good. Of course, when I would hear that Jordan did something good, I would turn around and look.

It's funny because I wasn't the only mom who couldn't watch her son play. Some moms talked the whole time to distract themselves from worrying about their sons. One mom would play video games when her son was playing on the field. When he got off the field, she would look up and really get into watching the game.

After the game, Jordan was exhausted. Because

NFL GAME DAY

of the heavy traffic around the stadium, we would all ride together for home games, which gave us an opportunity to talk. Jordan always wanted to talk to his dad and ask how he played and what he could do differently to improve. After the two of them talked at length, then Jordan would ask me my opinion of the game. Here's how I evaluated his performance: If he scored a touchdown, got an interception, or blocked the man in front of him, then it was a good game to me. If the other team ran by him or if he had to chase them down, then it was not a good game. But most of all, if Jordan could walk and talk with nothing taped up, it was a good game.

We just really tried to create a routine and something that would be memorable. We started while he played in college, and we kept that tradition going. These rituals and pregame routines were very important to me. You just don't know what's going to happen, because football is so unpredictable. You can be watching and see your son fall down, or a freak accident could occur. Anything could happen.

I just wanted to make sure Jordan could see that his family was there to support him. At every game, I wanted to give him a hug, and say, "I love you, son."

THE RIGHT MINDSET

*"So we fix our eyes not on what is seen,
but on what is unseen, since what is seen is
temporary, but what is unseen is eternal."*
—2 CORINTHIANS 4:18[8]

REMAIN HUMBLE

Your son has earned a spot on the 53-man roster, and he is officially a professional football player in the NFL. It is so important to help your son really manage expectations so he doesn't believe all the hype as he moves from college to the professional level. Playing at this level requires your son to have the right mindset to be able to handle the limelight, the pressure, the victories, and the setbacks that come as part of this opportunity. Give your son praise, but also give him honest feedback, because he's not always going to have the best day. Help your son manage all the attention, and help him remain humble.

One of the greatest challenges for a player is to watch a showboat on the team get all of the media hype and attention. We would constantly remind Jordan that the attention the showy player was getting may not last long-term, and that it could just be for a brief moment in time. It's hard for a young, impressionable player to remain humble when he sees that showy player getting his name called to suit up and his name is splashed everywhere. We advised Jordan to look at the big picture.

"Son, when you look back five years from now, typically you find that things have really gone downhill for certain players. You have to focus on long-term goals and the things that are unseen."

We advised Jordan of our expectations for how he should celebrate if he scored a touchdown. My husband told Jordan, "I don't ever want to see you showboating at the end of the field. I want you to celebrate because you did a good job, but you're not the team. It took the whole team to score that touchdown. So you're not going to go down into the end zone and do a little dance that draws attention to you. Be happy. Celebrate. Then get your butt back on the sidelines."

Even now, when Jordan watches a football game, he'll say, "Dad would have had a fit if he saw me doing some of those antics on the field."

We wanted to make sure he remembered that he

THE RIGHT MINDSET

was given a special gift. Yes, Jordan worked hard to get where he was, but there were thousands of players who were just as good, and some of them may have been even better. The message was: "It's not about you." When you are on the field, it's about the team.

As he got older, Jordan understood the wisdom of our advice. Early in his career, he had a teammate who was very flashy and boisterous, got a lot of headlines in the newspaper, and was signed to a great contract. Now we don't hear anything about this young man except reports of the trouble this former player has gotten himself into.

It's hard, even as a parent, to remain focused on the team over self. Chuck would look at me from time to time and say, "We are telling Jordan not to do any shenanigans on the field and to be respectful on and off the field, while it looks like the players who act up are having all the success and Jordan is really not."

That's when you have to reaffirm your beliefs as a parent and trust that you are guiding your child in the way that he should go. Teach your son to focus on something beyond this game and prepare him for the life that happens after his playing career is over. It may be really hard for your son to avoid the temptation to do stunts for attention and publicity, but you have to keep reinforcing to him the importance of exemplifying behavior that people will admire long after his time in the NFL has ended.

THE 50-YARD LINE MOM

GIVE YOUR SON CONFIDENCE

If you think about it, NFL players are told what to do every day. They have a playbook that tells them what to do in any given situation on the field. They have a structured schedule of what time to get up, what to eat, and when to do their workouts each day. They may also have an agent who is telling them what to do. A player's life is very structured and routine.

When a player has to make decisions, the process may be more difficult because of the insecurities he may have. The fears in a young player's head can be a source of embarrassment. He may perceive his fears as a sign of weakness, and weakness in football is not tolerated. So if a player is unsure or not quite confident about something, it's always good for that player to have his mom around to support him and give him reassurance on a regular basis.

Support your son by helping him feel confident in difficult situations. Just looking at these big, burly athletes may give you the impression that they are full of confidence, but sometimes these players are not as confident as they appear. They may need someone to assure them that they are smart and can make good decisions. There is not a better person to fulfill that role of encourager than you as his mom.

It can be tough for a rookie player to make an unpopular decision. For example, if he gets injured, will he have the confidence to say that he's not ready to play if he doesn't feel like he's fully recovered?

THE RIGHT MINDSET

Especially when the coaching staff, medical team, media, and fans are pressuring him to get back on the field quickly? Most players would probably tell themselves, *"I'm going to play anyway because I'm afraid of what will happen if I don't—losing my starting spot, dropping to the bottom of the depth chart, or getting cut from the team."* I would often tell Jordan to make the tough decisions and that I would support him.

Jordan knew his body better than anyone else. He could determine where he was physically. I wanted him to learn to trust himself and his decisions. What a player needs in many cases is reassurance that if he makes a tough decision, he will have someone in his corner backing him up. It's an ongoing process. Sometimes adversity will strike. During those times, it's important to provide reminders that God has a plan for his life and a timeline. Even when times are tough, your son has to stay true to who he is as a person, stay strong in his beliefs and values, and protect his health and well-being.

MANAGING DISAPPOINTMENTS

At some point, every athlete feels anger, frustration, or disappointment. These feelings can be the result of losing a big game or having to sit out while another player starts. Maybe he didn't play well, despite his best efforts. Our job as parents is to validate these feelings and let our sons know there's truth to them. You have to acknowledge the disappointment and get him to understand his role in it, because typically there is something that he did that contributed to the issue, or something he can improve upon. Then you have to lead your son to come to his own conclusions.

I helped my son manage the disappointments of playing pro ball by being available to him. I would ask Jordan to tell me what was going on, what was happening with the team, and how he was feeling. Then I would just listen. He would share his concerns, whether it was about not getting enough playing time, or feeling discouraged because he was working hard every day yet someone else was slated to start ahead of him, or his feelings about being third string on the depth chart.

Then I would ask Jordan, "Why do you think this is happening?" It's important to probe to see if the player has contributed to the current situation.

"Were you going to practice every day? Were there days you slacked off? Did you tick off the coach?"

Chuck was really good at the next step in the process. He would say, "Tell me some of the things that you plan to do about it."

We could have told Jordan, "This is what you need to do..." but, unless he bought into it and felt like it was partly his idea, he wouldn't really be on board. He might have done what we suggested, but his heart might not have been in it. We would only give our opinion after hearing his thoughts. Then we might suggest additional considerations for him to reflect on.

THE RIGHT MINDSET

Over time, it got to the point that Jordan would say, "You know when the coaches got all over me about something, I would tell them, 'Yes, I messed up, but Coach, you won't have to worry about that again. So what do you want me to do now?'"

In the pros, rejection comes in the form of being cut from the team. Football is a business. It's a major corporation, and sometimes they have to let people go and reorganize. Working in corporate America, I get that and understand it. All a player typically thinks, though, is, *"The team didn't want me even though I know I can do this."*

That first cut was so tough, and Jordan was cut a total of three times over the course of his NFL career. It never got any easier for him to accept being cut from a team. My husband would tell Jordan, "When you've done everything you can do and you've created a plan for where you want to go next, then it is what it is. Move on."

At times like this we really didn't have any answers. When frustrated or angry, an athlete's mind can become glued to the past. You want to help your son focus on the present and not dwell on the past. Young players must learn to move on to the next play, shot, routine, point, or opportunity. Your son needs to persevere and continue to work hard. He can overcome a lot of adversity by staying focused on his ultimate dream.

THE INJURED ATHLETE

Injury is almost certain in the NFL. Two weeks into the 2015 season, approximately 15% of all NFL football players had already suffered an injury. During the 2013–14 season there were more than 1,300 injuries, including 87 concussions.[9]

BE AN ADVOCATE FOR YOUR SON

In football, a player is told from a very young age that he has to be strong. I am sure your son has been told for years to pick himself up, dust himself off, and keep going. So he's learned to fight through adversity, setbacks, and disappointments. He has had to learn to fight for what he wants, against all odds.

A young NFL player competes for his job on

every play, every single day. At any point in time, he may be only one play away from the end of his career or one season away from a new rookie coming in and taking his place. The threat of an injury at any moment is always looming over his head. Will the injury slow him down, drop his stock with the team, or even worse, end his career?

One of the greatest challenges in working with the coaches and team doctors is that they are about the business of football. They are interested in player safety, but their focus may be more on quick player recovery than long-term player health. There is a delicate balance between player safety versus the chance of chronic injury, so the player has to understand his body.

You hope that these young men are at an age where they understand the consequences of going back out onto the field before they are ready and fully healed after an injury. Typically, they don't. That's where you as his mom can step in to advocate on his behalf.

When Jordan played in the NFL, I had introduced myself to the team doctors so that if Jordan got hurt, I was at least familiar with the physicians on the sideline. Jordan was a grown man now, so it was different than when he was playing football in high school and college.

At those stages of his life, I was the parent who made decisions on his behalf and asked all the questions. Now, my role had shifted to be more in the background, but it was just as important. You need to become aware of any pertinent medical information and share that information with your son.

Let me give you an example of what I am talking about: If your son breaks an arm or dislocates his shoulder, you should understand what the typical treatment for that injury is. Here are some possible questions you need to ask:

If someone has a dislocated shoulder, do they go right back out and play?

What type of medication is typically prescribed?

Was the medicine administered, and if so, how much and when?

These are just a few of the things your son needs to know. You have to be an advocate for your son. A mom will play that role in different ways, based on the parent-child relationship you and your son have. That relationship determines what your son will allow you to do for him or on his behalf, and it's different for every family. Find your role as part of your son's team, and then do your job to help protect his health and well-being.

CONCUSSION

Let's say your son is taken out of a game because he has a concussion. You need to know what the signs and symptoms of a concussion are. But you also need to know the signs and symptoms of recovery or non-recovery from a concussion, in case the team doctors clear him to play before he is ready. If you notice that he is still glazed, a little off-balance, or if he is still complaining about headaches and can't focus, then he has *not* recovered. The signs and symptoms of that concussion are still there.

Professional football is one of the few industries in which an injury can send you to the bottom of the list. You might not have a job, and with very few exceptions, you aren't going to be the starter. You are starting at the lower rank, and you have to come back up. That pressure is the reason why many NFL players go back on the active roster before they are ready. I can't even imagine how a player could be ready to go back onto the field the week after being diagnosed with a concussion.

Think about this: In boxing, a fighter may sustain a concussion every time he fights. Someone gets knocked out. Getting knocked out is a concussion, a severe concussion. A boxer is being hit in the head repeatedly. So what's different between boxing and football? A boxer may not go out and box again for six months to a year. There is time for healing.

The work that is currently being done on concussions is phenomenal. The latest research shows that there is a protein that develops in your brain when you suffer a concussion. The longer you allow your brain to heal, the more that protein level decreases. It is similar to healing from a broken arm. After eight weeks with good physical therapy, a broken arm heals and you can go out and play like it's never been broken. Is it possible that the brain works the same way? If you give your brain long enough to heal, can you go out and play like you never had a concussion?

I think longer recovery times don't happen because the players are so afraid of losing their jobs.

WHEN A DEVASTATING INJURY HAPPENS

During Jordan's fourth year in the league, he had come home for the weekend from OTAs (official training activities), which are off-season NFL training sessions. My husband and I were getting ready to go on vacation the next day because it was Memorial Day weekend. We were driving to Sandestin, Florida, with Dominique for the week. Jordan wasn't going with us because he needed to get back to camp to resume OTAs.

A few days earlier, Jordan had called to tell me that he was not feeling well. His ears were bothering him, so the trainers had given him antibiotics to treat an ear infection. I told him that feeling a bit off-balance was pretty typical for an ear infection and that it was normal. Although he said it had been going on for a couple of days, he seemed to be okay when he got home on Friday afternoon. Because he said his ears were still bothering him and his balance was off a bit, I told him that he probably needed to go back to the doctor and get checked out.

On Saturday, as we were driving through Alabama headed to Florida, Jordan called. "Mom, my ears are still hurting and the room is just spinning around and around. I'm scared. I don't know what to do," he said. "I had to crawl to get to my phone."

"Jordan, call 911 and have them come take you to the hospital," I said.

Jordan had to crawl down the stairs in his home to open the front door to let the paramedics in. He was put on a stretcher and transported to the hospital. The emergency room physicians diagnosed him with a severe case of labyrinthitis, a severe type of ear infection that causes equilibrium issues. They gave him some steroid shots and medicine for the vertigo and nausea.

I called my neighbor and asked if she could meet Jordan at the hospital since I was en route to Florida. I told her that Jordan had an ear infection and a really bad case of vertigo. When Jordan was released, my neighbor and her husband decided to take Jordan home with them because he was so dizzy.

Once we arrived in Sandestin, I called to check on him. They said Jordan was doing a little bit better. I asked if I needed to come home, but my neighbor and Jordan both said he was okay, even though he was still dizzy.

The next day, when I called to check on Jordan, once again the neighbor reported that he was still pretty dizzy. Jordan got on the phone and said he wasn't feeling well, so I decided that I needed to go home. I left Chuck and Dominique in Sandestin and flew back to Dallas. When I arrived at my neighbor's house, I couldn't believe the condition Jordan was

THE INJURED ATHLETE

in. He was slumped over in a chair, unable to sit upright. My neighbor had Jordan lie down and rest, but it didn't seem like he was getting any better. Jordan didn't want them to call me, because he hated the idea of me cutting my vacation short to come back home.

Jordan's vertigo was so severe that he was still unable to sit up. I literally had to walk him to the car because he couldn't walk unassisted. Thankfully, my neighbor lived right around the corner, so we didn't have that far to go to get home.

His condition was so bad that I had to walk Jordan to and from the bathroom. I kept thinking to myself, *"What on Earth has gone wrong here?"* I called the doctor who told me to bring Jordan into his office first thing Monday morning. I sat up with Jordan most of the night and took him to the doctor the next day. When the doctor saw Jordan, he was so concerned that he immediately took Jordan to see a neurologist. A variety of diagnostic tests and head scans were run, but they really didn't have any answers at that point.

The doctors said that Jordan had one of the most severe cases of labyrinthitis that they'd ever seen. They prescribed more steroids and an IV. I took Jordan home, and when he woke up the next day, he said, "Mom, I can't hear out of this ear." I became very alarmed.

Jordan was seen by an ear, nose, and throat doctor who confirmed that Jordan did indeed have hearing loss, but they were going to try to do everything possible to regenerate his hearing. Three steroid shots were injected directly into his ear over the course of a week and a half to try to reverse the damage. In the meantime, Jordan was supposed to have returned to camp.

This ear infection happened right after Jordan had an outstanding performance in OTAs that the team was really excited about. They planned for him to be the starter when the season kicked off. We had to tell the team that he wouldn't be returning to OTAs, but we fully expected that he would report on time for training camp, which was slated to begin in two weeks.

During those two weeks, Jordan went to two different specialists to receive the steroid injections in his ears, but his equilibrium was still way off. The doctors' prognosis was dire. They didn't think Jordan would ever be able to play football again because he was always going to have a vertigo issue, and he couldn't hear out of one ear. Jordan's response was, "In my position, I really don't need to hear. It's based more on hand signals and I still have hearing in one ear." Believe it or not, there are quite a number of football players who have suffered hearing loss. One of his teammates was nearly deaf in both ears, wore hearing aids, and had been playing professional football for years.

I asked Jordan, "Do you want to quit? You can't be out there with your balance off-kilter."

His answer was a vehement "No!"

Now the time had come for Jordan to report

THE INJURED ATHLETE

to training camp, but his balance was still off. He reported back a little bit early, and I took off from work and went with him. I couldn't let him go back by himself. He needed to get on a plane, and we didn't know what was going to happen. Once we landed, Jordan at first thought he was okay to drive. But a few moments later, he changed his mind and said that I needed to drive.

The next morning, Jordan decided that he was feeling okay and would drive himself to training camp because it was only five minutes away. Around noon, Jordan called to let me know that one of his teammates was driving him home. Jordan's balance was off, and it wasn't safe for him to drive.

It was a miracle that Jordan was able to complete training camp. Thankfully, the first week, the drills were pretty light. His coordination came back because he worked at it. He was back playing the game he loved, but it wasn't good enough. The team dropped him to third string.

Jordan went from being the starter for the upcoming season to now being third string as a result of an illness, something that was totally out of his control. He was still able to play, but the message was clear: You can't get ill. This downgrade in the depth chart is one of the reasons why so many players may fake their recovery. They know this could happen to them.

Jordan ended up playing half of the season that year, but then he got cut. He couldn't understand how he could go from being a starter, to third string, to being cut from the team. The team cut him, but then they brought Jordan back the very next week when another player got injured. When the team called him back to go play in Denver, they didn't even have a seat on the plane for him. It was insulting.

Jordan had a spectacular play that game against the Denver Broncos where he intercepted a pass from Peyton Manning. It was awesome. The following week, the team cut him again. By this time, there were only about three weeks left in the season. That's when Jordan got picked up by the New Orleans Saints. He ended up going to the playoffs with the Saints when they played the Seattle Seahawks.

As his mother, this whole ordeal was probably the worst part of Jordan's NFL career. My son was basically helpless, and I couldn't do anything for him. I went to every doctor's appointment with him and saw him get his hopes up. Each time he would go for a hearing test, he would say, "Mom I think I can hear something." He would get so excited. This rollercoaster of emotional heartbreak and hope went on for two years. Jordan never regained hearing in that ear, and he wears a hearing aid now.

The helplessness that you feel as a mother when something traumatic happens to your child is unfathomable—in or outside of sports. It's clear that it was divine intervention that he was able to go back and play at all after the ear infection, because the doctors didn't think he would. Jordan's absence during the preseason, because of the ear infection, had a huge impact on his career and with the team. The worst

THE INJURED ATHLETE

part is that there was nothing that I, as a mom, could do about it. I can't even imagine if it had been something more tragic. As a nurse, my whole career had been devoted to nurturing and caring for others, yet I couldn't help restore my own son's health.

The industry is so cut-throat. That's why so many players hide their injuries and minimize the pain that they're in.

It would be gratifying to see the NFL make changes to give players the job protection benefits that are common with many other corporations. I work in corporate America now, and if I fall and break my leg while I am traveling for work, my job is guaranteed until I can heal and return to work. A reasonable time frame for recovery from a medical injury is allowed. I can focus on recuperating and healing, and I don't have to worry about my livelihood.

An NFL player shouldn't be fearful of losing his job because he sustains an injury or becomes ill while doing his job.

THE FOOTBALL PLAYERS HEALTH STUDY AT HARVARD UNIVERSITY

After Jordan's hearing loss, I became even more passionate about being an advocate for player health. As an advocate for my own son, as well as having a heart for other players in the league, it was an honor to be invited to participate in the Football Players Health Study at Harvard University. I serve in the role as

Family Advisor, along with other family members, former players, and Harvard scientists and lawyers.

This landmark study is the largest study of its kind on living former players. The Football Players Health Study at Harvard University is collecting data from thousands of former and professional football players to better understand the effects that their football careers have had on their long-term health status. Another element that makes this research unique is that players are being studied from a holistic perspective over their life span, and not just for one health condition. The goal is to improve the physical and mental health of former players and positively impact the health of future players. The study is independent and free of influence from the NFL or the NFLPA.

Player input is coupled with Harvard scientists' research to address a variety of topics regarding player health. Studies are being conducted for new diagnostic, preventive, and state-of-the-art treatments that could positively impact player health. Legal and ethical aspects effecting player health are also being examined and recommendations are being developed to resolve these key issues. Other studies are being conducted on players' health status and quality of life.

This comprehensive, holistic approach is why I am so passionate about the Football Players Health Study at Harvard University. I am hopeful that the results from this Harvard University research will positively impact the game and improve players' long-term health. I want to see football continue and become a better, safer game.

LIFE AFTER FOOTBALL

"It appears that athletes who develop greater emotional intelligence are more likely to succeed in life."[10]

AFTER YOU STOP PLAYING, WHAT DO YOU DO?

Your job as Mom is to help these young professional athletes understand how to make the most of their opportunities. The day your son gets drafted is the day your son should begin planning for life off the field. Professional football is a means to an end, but it is not the end. Unfortunately, when a lot of young men leave the league, it is the end, in a way.

When a career in the NFL comes to a close, so many players are lost because that's all they've known. From middle school through high school and college, promising athletes are highly competitive,

THE 50-YARD LINE MOM

judged on their performance, and pursued for what they can bring to an organization. They are pushed to excel in sports, but once they've made it into the highest echelon of athletics, they are not coached on how to thrive in life.

I recently watched a sports program about a former NFL superstar. Early in his career, he broke his leg. The coaching staff and owner wanted to give up on him and replace him with a healthier player. This man said he was so depressed at the time that he thought about committing suicide because football was his life.

If he couldn't play professional football, he didn't want to live.

Oh, my goodness. How do you get to the point that you only value yourself if you are playing that sport? All of the hype, the fame, and notoriety surrounding professional football is partly to blame. To counteract this effect, we would mention other things to Jordan that he was good at while he was still playing ball.

"Son, you should go into broadcasting. You are great at it." Or, "You're a great speaker, so think about becoming a motivational speaker."

It was important to point out those other talents and skills. So when Jordan left the NFL, he was already working towards something else. Football may consume your son's life during a particular time, but you want to plant seeds to let him know that he is more than a football player.

The transition after being cut was tough on

LIFE AFTER FOOTBALL

Jordan. For a while, he would say, "Mom, I know I can play, but I'm not getting a call. I go to all of these workouts, but nothing comes of it."

He probably went to five or six workouts after he got cut from the New Orleans Saints. He went to Chicago, Atlanta, and Denver. Everyone was telling him he was wonderful, but no teams were calling him back. Jordan would question himself and wonder what it was that was holding him back. All the while, he continued to let us know he just wanted to play ball.

Jordan struggled, but he learned to adapt, and now he has moved on. The transition to life after football was not easy. A player needs someone to encourage him and let him know that he has more to offer the world than just playing professional football. Jordan needed me, his mom, in his life to keep nurturing him and to keep saying, "Son, let's take a look at what else you can do while you're waiting to get a call from another NFL team. Go down to the studio and do your radio show. Do you understand how good you are? The radio station called you back three times and now you have a local show, so it proves you can do other things and be successful."

It also helps if your son has a significant other who also sees his potential and speaks about it in an encouraging and supportive way. You want your son to find a woman who is pulling stuff out of him that he didn't know he had. "Jordan you had a wonderful game, but you know what I noticed that you're really good at? You would make a great speaker, if you think you would enjoy that."

So then the player can think, *"You know, I never thought about that."* Then, if the player tries it and loves it, he has found a new life and identity outside of playing professional football.

When you hear about former players committing suicide, getting into trouble, destitute, or living on the streets, you can understand it because it is so overwhelming for them. A talented athlete has to have the ego to play ball. Everybody gets so caught up in the allure of professional football, including the fans, that people forget there is a human there, a person. Behind that player, there is a family who is transitioning to life after the NFL right along with him.

CELEBRITY STATUS FALLS AWAY

I think for most athletes, their celebrity status starts when they're in college. That's when I really started seeing it appear. I think the greatest challenge after you leave the profession is no longer having that recognition.

I would watch Jordan when we would meet up with him the night before a game. We would go to a restaurant and fans would recognize him. Next thing you know, he's signing autographs. Then the next day, he leaves the game and little kids and their families are jumping around screaming and calling to him to please give them a signed autograph. At the time, Jordan would grumble a little. "Oh man, I

LIFE AFTER FOOTBALL

have to sign another autograph. I get so tired of this."

I would say, "Son, there will be a day when no one will want your autograph. This is an honor. If I'm in your presence, you're going to sign some autographs. You don't know what a privilege it is that someone would even want it."

When he would come back home to Dallas, friends, acquaintances, or family members would trip over me to get to Jordan. They wanted to be in his presence, to take pictures with him, ask questions, and have him tell them about his NFL experiences. Or we would go to a family reunion and all the attention would be focused on Jordan. An NFL player gets very accustomed to that attention.

The first year out of the league, he was still "Jordan Pugh the Celebrity." He was still getting invited to special events and celebrity get-togethers. Jordan was hanging out with some pretty high-profile celebrities, actors, and musicians. He would get invitations while he was on the team to special movie screenings, special parties, shows, and more.

The second year out of the league, it was like, "We'll invite so and so, and oh yeah, we'll invite Jordan Pugh, too." By the third year, Jordan could go to any restaurant he wanted to and walk right in without being noticed. Except for extremely high-profile players, people don't pay much attention to former NFL players for long. By this point, the invitations to special events have really slowed.

Jordan's experience was a little bit different because he was still broadcasting on the radio, but

THE 50-YARD LINE MOM

the invitations were nothing like they once had been. By then, family members weren't calling and asking for information about Jordan, and they no longer wanted his autographs and pictures.

It is a tremendous adjustment, and it can be an adjustment for the parent, too. I've watched how there would be crowds of people clamoring around the celebrity player's mom. But if the player had a bad year, that crowd moved on to the next hot player in the league, leaving the mom to wonder what happened. She thinks, *"Last year, I couldn't pick up my phone, I couldn't walk into a hotel lobby, I couldn't do anything without being surrounded by crowds of people. Now there's no one around and nothing going on."*

I can't tell you how many people would come up to me and ask, "Are you Jordan Pugh's mom? Can I get your autograph?"

I would be a little taken aback. "*My* autograph? You want *my* autograph?"

I became "Jordan Pugh's mom." That's why it's so important to make sure that you balance all of this with a level head, and don't lose your sense of self. You have to maintain your own identity. If you aren't careful, you will get caught up in your son's career, and his identity will start to meld into yours.

The worst place for me was in the workplace. I would go to work and people would make a point to mention that Jo Ann Pugh's son plays in the NFL. It was all they talked about. They would ask all of the time how he was doing. At first, I felt honored that my co-workers would even remember or think

LIFE AFTER FOOTBALL

about him. But then I began to think, *"I am not just Jordan Pugh's mom."*

The first year Jordan was out of the league, people would still ask me what was going on with Jordan. The second year, questions became more like, "How is your son doing?" "What is he up to now?" By the third year, no one asked about him at all. So it can be very deflating if you get caught up in being the star at the office.

There was a time when I used to walk into the corporate office and everyone gravitated towards me and pulled at me because they thought it was the greatest thing that I had a son who played professional football. Then, when his NFL career was over, all that attention stopped. If you don't have your own identity, you may go through the same withdrawals from the attention and adulation that your son may be experiencing.

There's another reason why I say that we're all drafted into this profession. When your son is living the high life, you're up there with him. And when your son is going through a low point, you're in the valley with him. You all have to prepare yourself for life after professional football.

Playing in the NFL will be a very short period of your son's life. Even if he has a long career by NFL standards, which is around 13 years, that means he will only be in his early 30s when he's done playing football. With the average person living into their 70s, what is your son going to do for the next 40 years of his life? He may want to start a business, but no one may want to do business with him if he was in jail, if he got into trouble often, or if he made poor decisions. That reputation will follow him.

People will praise him while he's running up and down the field, but they will forget about him the minute he gets off the field. Remember, it only takes about three years after he leaves the NFL before people won't remember his name and stop talking about him. We know players who have been inducted into the NFL Hall of Fame, and when I mention their names, people don't know who they are. They'll say, "Really? Who's that? He's in the Hall of Fame?"

Chuck and I were talking recently, and I asked him to name who the starters were in the Super Bowl this past year. He had to stop and think about it. Then he said, "Wait a minute, I need to think of which teams played in the Super Bowl last year." Chuck is a big football fan and even he struggled to recall both the teams and the starting players!

You might be able to remember the starting quarterbacks for the teams in the Super Bowl. Maybe someone will recall the MVP (most valuable player), but that's about it. It doesn't matter if these players played brilliantly. It doesn't matter if it was an outstanding, well-matched game. All of it is quickly forgotten.

The lesson is that even when you get to the pinnacle of your career and achieve the greatest success, people still forget about you. I can't stress enough how important it is that you and your son are constantly thinking about life after the NFL.

THE FOOTBALL NETWORK

"A mother is the truest friend we have, when trials heavy and sudden fall upon us; when adversity takes the place of prosperity; when friends desert us; when trouble thickens around us, still will she cling to us, and endeavor by her kind precepts and counsels to dissipate the clouds of darkness, and cause peace to return to our hearts."
—WASHINGTON IRVING

BUILD A STRONG NETWORK

It's good for your son to be visionary and understand that football is a short-term opportunity. If we go back to statistics, very few players get beyond two years in the league. There are a handful of players who are fortunate enough to play for 10 or more years, but most NFL players do not. The importance of building a great network is vital. Unless you've lived it, you cannot quite understand what it is like.

I can talk to my family or my close friends, but they can't relate. "Why are you upset? What's the issue? It sounds trivial. Your son is playing professional football, how bad can it be?" They just don't understand some of the challenges.

You will have family members asking you for things because they think that you, as the player's mom, have the money that your son has. It's my son who plays in the NFL, *not* me. The perception is that if your son is on the field, then he must be rich. Many people think the perceived wealth also applies to the family. Here's a good example of what I mean…

One year, we went back home for a family event. At the time, Jordan had been in the league for about four years. A family member said to me, "I figured that you all would be driving up here in a Maybach." (That's a top-of-the-line Mercedes.)

I said, "Oh really? What makes you think that?"

"You have a son who has been in the league for four years, so he must be rolling in dough by now."

I couldn't believe it. We drove the same car we bought when Jordan was in high school—well before he got into the league. Jordan did not buy our car, but family, friends, business acquaintances, and co-workers think I have a nice car because my son bought it.

THE FOOTBALL NETWORK

People don't understand what it's like to be a professional athlete until they've lived it. It can help to have a peer-to-peer network so you can talk through your experience with other people who truly understand the things you're going through. They become part of your trusted network. For me, it was helpful to speak to moms of other players. There was a special camaraderie in that we were all going through the same things—struggling to balance the needs of our families as well as parenting our other children to the best of our abilities. At the time, I felt like I was the only person in the world in my situation. But the truth is, my experience wasn't really unique. Being able to share my experiences with people who were in the same situation made the process a lot easier.

THE 50-YARD LINE MOM

I hope the information, advice, and stories I have shared in this book have been helpful. When I began my football journey with Jordan, I had so many questions and was navigating uncharted territory all on my own. I know that I could have used the support and advice of other moms. That's why I created 50–Yard Line Mom—to provide education and support for parents and athletes at all levels of sports, including high school, college, and professional.

A universal truth is that "Mom" is the center of gravity for all aspects of a child's life, and that includes the child's participation in sports. So our mission is simple—to share insights and advice that will have a significant influence on the development of your child throughout his or her sports journey.

Key services of 50-Yard Line Mom include workshops, seminars, and tools to help you navigate effectively through the complex world of sports, customized consulting for individuals and organizations, and motivational speaking.

I invite you to visit me online at 50yardlinemom.com. You don't have to face this journey alone.

ENDNOTES

1 The Bible: New International Version. biblehub.com/niv/1_samuel/1.htm

2 NCAA Research, "Estimated Probability of Competing in Athletics Beyond the High School Interscholastic Level" http://www.ncaa.org/about/resources/research/probability-competing-beyond-high-school Updated: September 24, 2013

3 NFL Collective Bargaining Agreement, https://nfllabor.files.wordpress.com/2010/01/collective-bargaining-agreement-2011-2020.pdf August 4, 2011

4 Avery Stone, "Former NFL player Phillip Buchanon says his mom demanded $1 million after he was drafted" http://ftw.usatoday.com/2015/04/former-nfl-player-phillip-buchanon-says-mom-demanded-1-million April 15, 2015

5 Bill Briggs, "NFL Owners Won't Run Hurry-Up Offense vs. Players" http://www.nbcnews.com/id/41855264/ns/business-personal_finance/t/nfl-owners-wont-run-hurry-up-offense-vs-players/#.WBS2ujtDBFI Updated: March 2, 2011

6 Donna Rockwell and David C Giles, "Being a Celebrity: A Phenomenology of Fame," *Journal of Phenomenological Psychology* 40(2):178–210 October 2009

7 Heather Turgeon, "Why Traditions and Holidays Are So Important for Your Kids," https://www.babble.com/toddler/importance-family-tradition-routine-toddler-2/ 2012

8 The Bible: New International Version, biblehub.com/niv/2_corinthians/4.htm

9 Judd Legum, "Two Weeks into the Season, 15% of Football Players Have Suffered an Injury" https://thinkprogress.org/two-weeks-into-the-season-15-percent-of-football-players-have-suffered-an-injury-9a9a1d906cdf#.yro75secf September 21, 2015

10 Joshua Freedman and Marvin Smith, "Emotional Intelligence for Athlete's Life Success" http://6seconds.org/sei/media/WP-NFL-EQ.pdf May 1, 2008

ABOUT THE AUTHOR

Jo Ann Pugh is a mother, mentor, and advocate for the health and well-being of athletes at all levels. She is the founder of 50-Yard Line Mom®, an organization dedicated to helping families of athletes pursuing professional sports, and a Family Advisor for the Football Players Health Study at Harvard University.

A nurse and mother of NFL veteran Jordan Pugh, Jo Ann learned firsthand the challenges players face on and off the field while pursuing a place in the pros and as part of the league. Armed with insider information, invaluable experience, and a compassionate approach, Jo Ann set out to offer much-needed guidance to these athletes and their families.

As a speaker, consultant, and author of *The 50-Yard Line Mom: One Mom's Journey Through the*

THE 50-YARD LINE MOM

NFL and Beyond, Jo Ann shares her wisdom and advice for navigating the complex, demanding, and exciting world of sports with the mission to improve the financial, physical, and emotional welfare of players at all levels of their journey.

To learn more, visit 50-Yard Line Mom online at **50yardlinemom.com** and on Facebook.

Made in the USA
Coppell, TX
14 April 2023